Also by Ronald Hirsch

Making Your Way in Life as a Buddhist: A Practical Guide

We STILL Hold These Truths: Preserving the Heart of American Democracy for the 21st Century

The Self in No Self

Buddhist Heresies And Other Lessons of A Buddhist Life

Making the Path More Accessible

Ronald Hanh Niêm Hirsch

ThePracticalBuddhist.com Publishing

Published 2012 by ThePracticalBuddhist.com Publishing, Stuyvesant, NY 12173. U.S. © 2010-2012 Ronald L. Hirsch. All rights reserved.

No part of this publication may be reproduced, stored in a retrieval system, or transmitted in any form or by any means, electronic, mechanical, recording or otherwise, without the prior written permission of Ronald L. Hirsch

ISBN 978-0-9883290-0-3 (softcover), 978-0-9883290-1-0 (eBook)

To the Ven. Huyen Te and Ven. Thai Tue,
who imparted clear and insightful teaching
into the heart of the Buddha dharma,
revealing the path to end suffering.

TABLE OF CONTENTS

Preface		1
1	Life Before Buddhism – A Child Lost	5
2	First Things First – Building a Platform of Serenity	25
	I Believe – The Importance of Faith	33
	Aware Breath = Instant Samadhi	36
	The Power of Smiling Mindfully	39
	Take Joy in Each Moment, in Everything You Do	42
	Accepting Ourselves –	
	Cultivating a Compassionate Heart	45
	Accepting Life	52
	Staying Grounded	59
3	Coming to Understand the Fundamentals –	67
	Behind the Clouds the Sky Is Always Blue:	73
4	Breaking Through the Dogma –	85
	Buddhist Heresies:	
	The Self in No Self	91
	The Fullness of Emptiness	96
	The Right Way When There Is No Right or Wrong	100
	The Desire That Is Right Desire	104
	The Four Basic Needs and	
	Our Duty to Address Them	108
5	The Last Barrier – Surrendering the Ego:	115
	The Missing Noble Truth	
6	Finding Peace, If Not Enlightenment, and	121
	The Lessons of the Heart Sutra	
Epilogue – The Present		137

Preface

No matter how much we learn about the Buddhist path, ultimately it is for each of us to apply the lessons of the dharma to our often rather messy lives. In this book, I use my life as an object lesson on how we lose our true Buddha nature, the terrible impact that has on our lives, and how with much discipline and patience we can slowly open the gate to our true Buddha nature and finally be at one with it again.

Following the Buddhist path to end our suffering is no easy matter. Enlightenment for most of us does not come in a flash, if ever. For me, the deepening of my practice has been incremental, with each stage bringing with it greater awareness, clarity, and peace, even as my core "issues" and the suffering they caused me remained pretty much unaffected. Only in the last, or better put most recent, stage (for who knows what is yet to come), have the demons lying deepest in my gut been defanged. The feelings are still there ... they will always be there ... but they have lost their power over me so long as I am mindful and aware; when they arise now, I do not engage them, I do not attach, and they ebb slowly away.

The first problem we face is that our lives are filled with much conflict, anger, craving, frustration, and fear. We experience a state of anguish more often than we can bear. We want to experience peace, but when we read about enlightenment, it seems like a very far-off goal; indeed, it may not even be a goal at all, so impossible does it seem. And so for years/decades, we remain subject to the forces of our ego and the culture around us.

How then, I thought, can I achieve during this phase of my practice the serenity to provide at least a partial end to my suffering and the peace necessary to more deeply explore myself and the Buddha dharma?[1] The first collection of pieces, "Building a Platform of Serenity," suggests a practical, realizable approach.

Serenity is good ... far better than anguish ... but it doesn't relieve us of our suffering, so deep does it lie. To receive the benefits of the Buddha dharma, we need to go deeper into it and ourselves. The problem that many of us face, though, is that the most fundamental principles of Buddhism are so foreign to our way of thinking and to the culture we have grown up in that they can be difficult to comprehend even on an intellectual level, let alone internalize them and change the paradigms of our lives. And the teaching we receive often is of little help.

Faced with this barrier, Buddhism for many never gets far beyond the feel-good phase. But I was lucky. A very powerful teacher who hammered home the fundamentals came into my life, and later I arrived at my own understanding of them. The next chapter, "Coming to Understand the Fundamentals: Behind the Clouds the Sky is Always Blue" both shares the teaching I received and explains the fundamentals in a way every person can relate to, thus helping to dissolve the barriers to understanding.

But as the years passed, I encountered other barriers. At times it seemed like the more I learned, the more conundrums arose that frustrated progress on the path. Even advanced practitioners can find these conundrums difficult. For example, a Zen master, an obviously advanced student of Buddhism, found after 35 years of study that the Buddhist concept of no-self and the corresponding unity of all things left him feeling like "an invisible man," lacking perversely any feeling of unity with himself. And so he went

---

[1] The "Buddha dharma" refers to the teachings of the Buddha. At various points in the book I refer also to "dharma talks," which are talks given by teachers about some aspect of the dharma.

to see a psychiatrist! (see "Enlightenment Therapy," Chip Brown, *The New York Times Magazine*, April 23, 2009)

As another example, several years after beginning my practice of Buddhism, I asked a wise monk, who had received his dharma transmission from Thich Nhat Hanh, how to reconcile the Buddhist teaching of emptiness ... no right or wrong, no good or bad ... with the Five Precepts which set forth moral guidelines for Buddhists to follow.[2] His response was, "that's an interesting question." No answer, however, was forthcoming.

After 15 years of practice, I have found that in Buddhism as in most religions or philosophies there is a danger when received dogma is taken too literally and absolutely. Also, sometimes a semantics problem arises when an inadequate word or phrase has been used to translate a concept, creating a barrier through misunderstanding.

The conundrums we face thus arise not from the teachings of the Buddha; the problems arise from the way in which lesser mortals, even enlightened ones, have at times promulgated those teachings. The answer to seeming conundrums such as the two posed above lie within the Buddha dharma, carefully viewed. The title of the next selection of pieces, "Breaking Through the Dogma: Buddhist Heresies," thus does not reflect my view of my thoughts, but rather reflects how some in the Buddhist community may view them.

So after years of practice I gradually came to not just an understanding of the dharma, but was able to incorporate it into my daily life to at least some extent. But I

---

[2] The Five Precepts are rules or trainings, not imperatives like the Ten Commandments, that lay people vow to practice when they formally commit themselves to Buddhism. The ceremony is called, "taking the Precepts." Briefly stated they are: not killing, helping others, refraining from sexual misconduct, speaking and listening with loving kindness, and not consuming things which are harmful.

was limited in this because my ego was still a very active part of my life. We may be very aware of how what it's telling us is not in our best interest or a true reflection of reality, yet we remain helpless before its power. To make further progress on the path I needed to find an answer to the question, what to do with my ego?

Different teachers approach this matter in different ways. My two Vietnamese Zen teachers took a somewhat novel, for Buddhism, approach to this problem ... surrender your ego to your true Buddha nature. I describe this teaching in, "The Last Barrier – Surrendering The Ego: The Missing Noble Truth."

It is easier to receive wisdom, however, than make it yours and change the paradigms of your life. Even after years of practice, surrendering my ego to my true Buddha nature did not happen overnight or come easily. It was a long process. But with diligence, patience and continued practice we can find peace, if not enlightenment, and approach the state of perfected wisdom described in the Heart Sutra. The lessons of these years are described in the final chapter of the book.

Following the Buddhist path in any situation, even for a monastic, is not easy. Doing it while living in today's world with all of its stressors and ego triggers is even more challenging. Hopefully by addressing some of the barriers that people seeking to start or stay on the path often face in their practice, this book will make the path more accessible for the lay Buddhist.

Chapter 1
Life Before Buddhism – A Child Lost

1.

I'm looking at a photo of myself as a toddler … laughing, gigling. Wearing the white knit jacket that my mother made, my curly blond locks blowing in the wind, I am running across the field towards my father who is taking the photo. In my mind, though, I am running into my father's waiting open arms. When he lifts me up in the air saying, "There's my Ronnychen," I laugh as only a child can laugh, basking in the glow of my father's love.

. . . .

A sangha[3] member once remarked that, "Every person who walks through the doors of temple does so for the same reason … they are suffering and they are looking for a way to relieve their suffering." I was certainly no exception.

As I write this I am in the 67th year of my life with so much left to learn. Recently I've taken to looking at the photo album of the first years of my life, put together carefully by my father, the photos neatly attached to the black paper, the dates and places noted in his characteristic handwriting in white pencil. Everywhere I see images of a smiling, happy little boy; his proud, loving older brother; his attractive, kind, youthful mother; and occasionally, through

---
[3] The word "sangha" can be understood at several levels. In the West, it generally refers to the community of people who regularly attend a temple or more broadly to all Buddhist practitioners. The traditional usage refers more narrowly either to all ordained monks and nuns or to the group of practitioners who have attained a high level of realization.

the use of the camera's time exposure, a beaming happy father.

The laughter, the joy in the life shown on these pages is palpable. Yet it was soon gone, at least for me.

I cannot change the past, but I can observe it and myself with an aware mind and free myself from the past, from my learned experience, from my ego. And so, for the past 15 years or more, I have been following the Buddhist path, searching for my true self, my true Buddha nature.

During this time I've become aware of things I'd totally forgotten and things I was never aware of at the time. And things I've never gotten right. That ones perspective can be so wrong for so long with such devastating consequences to oneself is disheartening. What I thought was real was often illusion; what I thought was illusion was real. I'd always believed that I knew so much, and yet I've come to realize that in truth I know so little.

We all come to Buddhism bound by the chains of the past and our obsession with the future. But while the essence of our struggles is the same ... we suffer from self-doubt, craving, ignorance, and anger caused by the accumulated detritus of our life experience ... how each of us approaches Buddhism is largely determined by our natural temperament and how those experiences have shaped our personality. And so, I share with you now the relevant details of my life experience.

2.

My birth on January 11, 1944 was a joyous occasion. For my parents, who had immigrated to the United States from Nazi Germany via England in 1940, my birth completed their making of a family, which had been interrupted by the war. It was also another affirmation of their new life as Americans, as evidenced by the American flags and red, white, and blue ribbon that adorn the little framed birth announcement that they put together, and which I still have. For my brother Peter, who was born in Germany in 1935, my birth gave him the brother he had hoped for.

Like so many immigrants before and since, my father was a hard-working man trying to build a new and secure life for his family. He started from scratch, working as a truck driver for the man who sponsored the family's visa to immigrate to the U.S. Within a short time, he graduated to a salesman, and several years later opened up a new branch of the company in a nearby city, ultimately buying them out. He was in many ways the prototypical American success story, although he didn't feel like a success till quite late in life.

An extremely upright, principled, and intelligent man, my father was introspective. But at the same time he was a definite extrovert ... he loved talking and laughing with almost everyone. He truly liked people.

My mother was a perfect match...loving, serious yet fun-loving, a wonderful homemaker, and industrious (she knitted much of my baby and toddler clothing, made slipcovers and curtains, painted the inside of the house, and also earned some money knitting models for a local knitting company).

They were very much in love, as evidenced by the poems he wrote her on many occasions, from the early years of their knowing each other to their old age, as well as just their obvious physical chemistry. And that love was transmitted to my brother and me ... as well as their inner strength, their social conscience, and their belief in their fellow man, which never faltered.

By all accounts I was a very happy baby and toddler. In my baby book, my mother wrote that *"Ronny is a very good baby, no trouble at all, and always happy."* In a letter from my father many years later, he wrote, *"What a sunshine you always were."* My brother adored me (as I did him). My mother wrote in my baby book that my brother loved to sing and dance for me, and that I got especially excited when I would see my brother and loved him dearly. Indeed, through all the years, the two of us have remained very close and loving.

That happiness comes through clearly in the photos of me as a baby and toddler. Look at these photos and you'll see a child experiencing joy for no particular reason ... other than feeling secure and loved.

While there was definitely a side to my father that was about German strictness and discipline, he was a very warm, demonstrative, physical man who did not shy from showing his affections and feelings to family and friends, and he expected the same from my brother and me. One of the rituals of our household that continued till my father died was that when we would come down to breakfast, or in later years see him for the first time, we would kiss my father on his cheek.

When I was a few years old, I remember my father would come home from a long day's work, come to me in my bed, and play with my toes ... "This little piggy went to market, this little piggy stayed home, this little piggy worked in the garden, and this little piggy ran all the way home!" ... making me laugh and very happy.

While I otherwise have scant actual memory of my first 4 or 5 years, my acquired memory of those early years has an almost idyllic quality. The photos together with the stories of going to Green Lane in the summer to swim and picnic, skating on a frozen pond in the winter, going sledding, and many more point to a family who lived and played together.

3.

Then in 1948 we moved to Reading where my father had started a new business. And my world changed.

No longer was my father an integral part of my daily life because he wasn't physically there. The demands of his new business made it necessary for him to work 7 days a week, morning till late in the evening. I would only see him at breakfast, at weekend dinners and occasionally on Saturday night.

His absence was hard for me as a child to deal with. What made it harder was the quality of those fleeting moments when we were together.

I had by the time I was 6 or 7 become a fussy eater … that is to say, I cut the fat off of everything and was picky with my food. My father grew up during the deprivations caused by WWI … the food shortages were extreme. Dairy products and meat were almost non-existent. For his Bar Mitzvah, his mother had to bake him a cake using beans. For him, the trite phrase, "Think of the starving children in Europe," had real meaning. He was brought up to eat everything … *everything* …that was put before him; the plate had to be wiped clean.

So when he watched me night after night fuss with my food and leave things on my plate, he would literally get red in the face and very angry with me. With some frequency, he sent me to my room.

My eating habits bothered my father so much that he had my mother take me to our family doctor, saying (in my presence) that it wasn't normal. When my mother explained to the doctor how I ate, he informed her that this was very normal for a child, and that I actually ate much better than many children! My father was not mollified by the doctor's opinion.

In a child's world, events don't have to be horrific to leave everlasting scars that alter its life. I felt hurt and belittled. Years later I realized that I had interpreted my father's absence and his frequent anger with me as meaning that he didn't love me any more and that I took to heart his statement that I wasn't normal. Despite his other showings of affection and his support for me in various ways that were a positive influence on my development, I felt unloved and was desperate to be loved by him. I ceased being a happy child.

The other change in my world came about when I started school. Suddenly I was thrown together with many children, especially boys, my own age. And it quickly became very clear to me that I was different from them. Perhaps even more importantly, the other boys realized that I was different from them too.

I was no rough and tumble, typical American boy. I didn't horse around; I didn't play sports; I was more quiet and studious. I was also the shortest kid in my class. To top it all off, as was noted by my mother in my baby book at age 6, "*He prefers to play with girls.*" And then as an afterthought, she crammed in the parenthetical phrase "*(occasionally)*" under the line. (I did indeed enjoy playing with some of the neighborhood girls, although this stopped when I finally started making friends with some boys in school.) I also wore frequent hand-me-downs from my male cousin who lived in England ... where the coats buttoned on the opposite side, like girls' in the U.S. I remember one time some of the neighborhood boys asking my mother, "*Why does Ronny wear girl's clothes?*"

I experienced the impact of being different in several ways. Certainly I was very aware of this during recess on the playing field. No one ever wanted me on their team ... I was not an asset that would help them win.

But the exhibition of disdain for me by some of the rougher boys did not stop with this mild form of social ostracism. It turned physical and abusive. One incident involved my next-door neighbor who was a year older than

I ... in the playground, he held my arm fast while he harshly rubbed sand into the top of my hand, making the skin raw, while verbally abusing me. Another time, one of the boys hit me in the stomach on the way home from school and knocked the wind out of me.

Then, one warm, late spring day on the way home from school, several of the neighborhood boys ... a couple older, a couple my age ... grabbed me and took me to a vacant field. There they stripped me, held me down, and peed all over me! I remember them shouting nasty things while they abused me, but don't remember the specifics. Then they ran off, leaving me there to pull myself together, get dressed, and go home.

To say that I, a 7- or 8-year old at that point, was traumatized by these incidents would be an understatement. To make matters worse, I kept the terrible last incident to myself. If my memory is accurate, while I informed my mother of the first two incidents, I never told her or anyone about the last one because it was so unbearably shameful. For at least a year after that incident, whenever I would walk home from school by myself, I would worry that the boys would snatch me again.

Before we moved to Reading, I was a happy child who saw the world through a child's innocent eyes and felt that his world and the love he was shown were secure. Now I began to see myself through the eyes of others ... in the case of my father, as one not deserving of love and not normal; in the case of a segment of my peers, as a freak, as someone below disdain, as someone socially undesirable. And I learned that love, even the love of a father, is often conditional. The elemental nature of these feelings would remain deep inside me throughout my adolescence and most of my adult life.

4.

Some children faced with such circumstances would just crawl into a hole and protect themselves through isolation and become depressed. But thankfully, the inner strength of character that I inherited from my parents or learned from them led me to take a very different path in the face of these problems.

My parents had always been very encouraging of my intelligence and abilities. Early on, I realized that if I focused on these assets, I could gain people's respect if not their love ... perhaps even my father's. How much of this was my own doing, and how much was at the prodding and support of my parents I really don't know. I do know that many years later, my father wrote to me, "*That you were physically smaller and daintier than your classmates must have often hurt you, but you did not show it, instead proved yourself spiritually and intellectually superior.*"

Unfortunately, I also developed a negative coping skill ... I acquired the defensive mindset of putting down those who disliked me as being lesser persons, as not being worthy of my friendship. And since I felt most people wouldn't like me because I wasn't normal, that mindset extended to most people with whom I came in contact. I only reached out to those who I somehow felt would react well to me.

Thus on the one hand, I created a persona that would eventually lead to professional success and a strong career. On the other hand, I developed a persona that doomed me to feel isolated from most of my peers. I would always have a small circle of close friends, but I would never experience the larger acceptance that deep down I craved.

Interestingly, only rarely during my life has someone whom I reached out to rejected me. Was this validation of my keen judge of character, or was it a sign that my rejection by others was a self-fulfilling prophecy? That if I had only reached out to others the way I did to people who I immediately felt comfortable with, I would have found the acceptance that I sought? It's a question I'll never know the answer to, although I suspect the truth lies somewhere in the middle.

The other aspect of my life that changed, or rather acquired a different emphasis, was my relationship with my mother. When I became emotionally distanced from my father, my mother became my emotional anchor and support ... she was always there for me, and her love was always self-evident and unconditional.

One of my favorite memories of this time is coming home from school each afternoon. I would open the front door, sing out "Yoo-hoo," and then head to the kitchen where my mother would either be ironing or cooking. As she worked, she listened to the soap operas then popular on the radio ... "The Lives of Helen Trent," "Pepper Young," and "Stella Dallas" ... and I would listen to those programs with her as I drank the milk and ate the piece of cake she had given me. I felt very safe in those moments.

But as close as I was with my mother, she never intervened in my problems with my father nor, that I can remember, countered the feelings that were developing inside me about my social undesirability.

5.

Asleep, unaware of the forces that were shaping my persona, and with the paradigms of my life pretty well set by the time I was 8 or 9, my life unfolded in not--surprising ways. Side by side I exhibited traits of normalcy, overachievement, and neurosis.

I excelled in school. I achieved high grades (my 7th grade math teacher, a kind man named Mr. Bierly, said to me once that, "Good things come in small packages.") and ended up graduating 2nd in my class.

I also became very active in school organizations ... everything from the high school band, to the National Honor Society, to Key Club. In my senior high school yearbook, there were more pictures of me in the book than anyone else because I was more active, and an officer in more organizations, than anyone. My efforts to gain the respect of my peers clearly worked. In my senior year, I even was on the newly formed wrestling team, which definitely got me some points with the guys.

But although my status had improved, and I had a few good friends, I still felt different ... and I still felt very insecure socially. That, together with my father's continuing angry reaction to my eating habits, resulted in an unfortunate syndrome.

Whenever I would be invited to a friend's house for dinner or would be invited to a dinner party (e.g. Bar Mitzvah), I would get nervous beforehand that I would not like what was being served me and thus offend my friend's parents. So nervous that I would get physically ill before the event and vomit ... and then not eat anything or just pick at my food at dinner!

This time my father really thought something was wrong with me, said so very bluntly to me, and sent me to a psychiatrist. The few sessions had no beneficial impact, although the connection to my father's outrage became very clear during the sessions.

This somewhat crippling syndrome, or at least embarrassing discomfort, continued well into my 20s. The last time it occurred, I was going to have dinner for the first time at the parents' home of a close friend. I was very nervous but didn't vomit. At dinner, I ate the spaghetti *very* slowly, breathing deeply. His father said, "What's the matter? You don't like pasta?" I could have died, but I kept on eating, cleared my plate, and that was the last time I had that discomfort. I guess I finally outgrew it somehow.

In September, 1961 I entered college. My first time away from home for an extended period was not easy for me. For the most part I floated through my college experience feeling almost invisible and not much a part of things. I did participate in some activities like the glee club and convocation choir (the latter of which I enjoyed very much, not just because of the wonderful music we sang, but probably because the other choir members were also on the geeky side), and of course went to football games and other sports events with the few friends I made. In my freshman year, I even trained to be a coxswain on the crew team but eventually dropped out. I was obviously making an effort to be a part of something, but I never felt really connected; I just went through the motions. My self-fulfilling isolation continued.

After college, I went to law school. In this new environment, more intellectually rigorous and serious, I not only prospered academically, but socially I started coming more into my own. For the first time in my life I was part of a larger group of people with whom I felt I had much in common and so I felt comfortable reaching out more. Here I found I was appreciated by people on multiple levels ... it wasn't just respect for my intelligence ... and I started to slowly blossom, becoming somewhat more aggressive socially, having more acquaintances. But even in this setting,

I still felt somehow undesirable to most and so confined my friendship to a relatively small group of people.

Over the next 25 years, my professional life developed steadily and I had a very varied, rewarding career. But since the details of my professional trajectory are not particularly relevant to the themes of this book, suffice it to say that after teaching law for a couple of years, I was a legal aid lawyer, a survey researcher, a nonprofit executive, and a consultant. I also had alternative careers as a composer and writer.

My professional career became a source of self-esteem. As the years progressed, I became more and more sure of myself. I conceived major projects that others often viewed as beyond reach, but if I felt they were possible, I went for them with all my energy and tenacity. I got better at interacting with people, at least in a professional setting. Even more importantly, I came into contact with a number of people through my work who became friends for life and who truly loved me.

But while I had plenty of evidence in my various jobs that I was valued and considered a desirable friend and colleague by those I was close to, and these relationships brought much joy into my life, there was also plenty of evidence that many people I worked with didn't take a liking to me or worse.

It seemed I had a problem in that I spoke my mind when asked ... if I had an opinion, which I did about most things, I would offer it unhesitatingly and with self-assuredness. Many people in the workplace did not react well to this. One person once said to me, "If you think you can say what you think around here, you're stupid!" And so, there was no shortage of incidents both in the workplace and in the larger social world to reinforce the old feeling that I was undesirable.

Since we tend to focus on what we want but don't have, my internalized negative feelings continued more or less unabated. The depth of my social insecurity and craving for acceptance was so great that the dislike or disinterest of the seemingly many trumped the love of the few. I was never far from such feelings.

6.

There is one more element of my life that is relevant for the reader's understanding of the conflicted feelings and depth of suffering I was experiencing when I found Buddhism.

As the reader may have guessed by now, I am gay. In my late teens and while I was in college, I became ever more aware that part of the difference I felt from my peers, and they from me, was of a sexual nature. Towards the end of law school, since I never had felt anything sexual towards the few girls I had dated, and since I was aware that I had a sexual attraction towards some men, I finally decided to act on it. The result ... I realized without question that I was gay.

And miraculously, I blossomed. The reader might think this odd ... that this should have added to all my insecurities. However, much of my feelings of social insecurity stemmed from the fact that as a child and adolescent I didn't understand why I felt different or was perceived as being different by my peers. For years, I thought there was something wrong with me; that I wasn't normal.

Once I self-identified as gay, I knew why I felt different and I felt good about it. Truly! Not for a moment did I have any shame about being gay, thanks to my upbringing and my parents' open, clearly non-judgmental, acquaintance with some gays. I knew in my heart that what mattered, certainly to my family, was who I was, not what I was. Being gay would not be deemed "not normal" by them.

Because my parents' attitude was certainly not the norm, a word of explanation. My parents came from a liberal German-Jewish background that truly believed that all people were equal and they acted accordingly. It didn't matter how rich or poor the person was, how smart or simple, what the color of their skin was ... all people were dealt with by my parents cordially as equals. And that included gays and lesbians.

But I digress. The other point is that when I was in a gay bar, I *wasn't* different from the other people who were there ... at least with regard to being gay; I had found my social/sexual peer group.

There were many other ways in which I was different, things I didn't have in common with my fellow gay bar-goers, but those were usually things I felt good about. And as for looks, it's not something I was very hung up on. I thought I looked nice ... and that was fine for my self-image. Tall, handsome, and buff was not what I needed to see in the mirror.

There were lots of people out there who I knew weren't right for me, and I knew the reverse was certainly true as well. My mother always said, "Better to have no relationship than a bad relationship." And I totally agreed; my standards were high. I was at a point in my life where I was able to be emotionally mature and reasonably objective about this issue. Not that there weren't times when I felt rejected.

Over the next two decades, I had several long-term relationships, each succeeding one of greater length and depth. My last ended after 12 years only because my partner died of AIDS. Throughout these years, my partners and I were shown love and affection by family and friends

How grateful I've always been that my family and friends were people to whom my being gay wasn't an issue. So often, people are faced with a stony silence or worse ... total rejection and ostracism and/or verbal abuse. I've never understood how parents can reject a child over his or her sexual orientation, but tragically it happens frequently, even in today's more enlightened age.

The reader may be wondering at this point, where's the conflict and suffering I mentioned at the beginning of this section? Despite all the positive things that my coming out did for me, all was not well.

7.

The room was dark and small ... the only light coming from the flickering images on the small video monitor of men having sex with men. The room smelled of cigarettes and sweat. I sat on a plastic chair ... quiet ... the excitement and animal passion of the previous 15 minutes gone. Gone also was the man with whom I had shared that excitement, a man whose name I did not know, a man I knew nothing about other than his physicality. After the intense high came a feeling of nothingness, a void ... I had not found whatever I was looking for. Instead, in an unkind irony, the feelings I was escaping from were reinforced. And so the cycle would continue. My next effort to escape would not have to wait for long. Such is the fate of a sex addict.

. . . .

When I began my life as a gay man in 1969, my psyche was still very much gripped by the feelings of social undesirability and the insecurity of love that I acquired as a child. Yes, I felt good about being gay, but those old feelings remained in my gut, transferred now to gay relationships.

The milieu I came out in was the heady post-Stonewall world of gay liberation, with anonymous sex available literally 24 hours a day in easy to access venues. And I responded to that world like a kid in a candy store. I couldn't get enough and I became a sex addict.

Sex and love addiction is a well-studied syndrome. As reported on MSNBC and in numerous publications, an estimated 16 million Americans suffer from sex addiction ... almost as many as alcohol addiction. Its psychological characteristics or causes are similar to those of other addictions. At their core, they all revolve around escaping from feelings of anxiety, loneliness, low self-esteem, and insecurity. Sex addiction is not about sex as such ... sex is just the medium for attempting to find validation. Even in a relationship, addicts fear abandonment and rejection, and so act out to escape from that fear. There is no logic here, just psychological fact.

And while psychological in nature rather than chemical, the grip, the control it has on ones life is as powerful as alcohol or drug addiction. And it is so degrading.

Of course, many participated in the hedonism of the early 70s. But whereas most soon tired of the empty highs of such sex and stopped, I became addicted to those highs. The easiness in this context of experiencing the illusion of being found desirable proved to be an intoxicating antidote, albeit only momentarily, to my craving for validation of social desirability and my insecurity in relationships. I engaged in this compulsive acting out behavior at every opportunity.

And so, side by side with my evolving relationships and otherwise stable life, I was secretly an increasingly out-of-control addict. My usually dependable will power was useless here. I tried numerous times to stop; I tried all sorts of mental tricks. But nothing worked.

This activity continued for almost 20 years. Then one day, a good friend of mine mentioned to me that he had started attending meetings of Sexual Compulsives Anonymous (SCA). I had never heard of the organization nor even the term, "sexual compulsive." But as soon as he told me a little bit about SCA, the light bulb went on in my head. "So that's why I've never been able to control my sexual acting out behavior," I said to myself.

The next week, I went to my first meeting in a nondescript storefront. I got to the meeting early, and as I sat there the room filled up with a wide assortment of gay men ... young and old, handsome and homely, kempt and unkempt. Visually, there was no norm. But regardless of background or present place in life, we were all there for the same reason.

To someone who is not an addict, it's hard to describe the effect that the meeting had on me. But as someone read the 14 "characteristics most of us seem to have in common," as the 12 steps were read, and as we read, in turn, paragraph by paragraph, a chapter from the "big book" which expands on the 12 steps, I recognized myself in all those words and saw a path out of my addiction. This was truth. And then to hear person after person, as we went around the room, speak to the problems they were having with their addiction, I knew that I was not alone.

As with any effort one undertakes, but even more so with personal psychological issues, dedication and commitment are essential to eventual success. Luckily, and I say that fully aware of the irony, I had hit bottom over the course of the previous half year. My compulsive acting out behavior was totally out of control; it was consuming large portions of my time, it was draining my energy, and it was degrading. Given my basic personality and desire for peace in my life, I was ready to make a real commitment. The time was ripe.

And so, over the course of the next 5 years until I moved away from Chicago, I attended the Monday night gay SCA meeting every week. And from the first meeting I went to, my acting out behavior was substantially reduced and my life began to be returned to me.

I had my slips (acting out on your bottom line) as most recovering addicts do, but after each occurrence I would recommit and start counting days all over again. As time went on, my slips grew less and less frequent even as my bottom line grew more encompassing, so infrequent after a few years that I stopped counting days. The norm was now not acting out in any way ... physical or virtual. The transformation was such a gift.

Somehow, the 12-step program is so empowering that it can alter deeply rooted destructive behavior if one is ready for it and has the necessary commitment. As we say in SCA, "The program works if you work it." I for one can certainly vouch for the truth in that. I am a grateful recovering sex and love addict.

It was also through my SCA experience that I first was exposed to a Buddhist perspective:

The Serenity Prayer: "Lord, grant me the serenity to accept the things I cannot change, courage to change the things I can, and wisdom to know the difference."

Acceptance: "And acceptance is the answer to all my problems today. When I am disturbed, it is because I find some person, place, thing, or situation – some fact of my life – unacceptable to me, and I can find no serenity until I accept that person, place, thing, or situation as being exactly the way it is supposed to be at this moment. ... Until I could accept my sexual compulsion, I could not stay sober; unless I accept life completely on life's terms, I cannot be happy. I need to concentrate not so much on what needs to be changed in the world as on what needs to be changed in me and in my attitudes."

Chapter 2
First Things First: Building a Platform Of Serenity

1.

Serenity. What a completely foreign concept this was to me. How can anyone be serene unless they're a saint? All I'd known in my life was constant inner turmoil, certainly since I was a young child. And in looking around at my peers and family, and at the images of the larger culture, I didn't see anyone who was serene. My parents may have been in love, and friends laughed and relaxed, but that's not serenity. Everyone was beset with problems that disturbed them. Even in the idealistic sitcoms of the 50s, whether it was the Beaver, or Ozzie and Harriet, or Lucy ... everyone's lives were filled with conflict and confusion. Yet I knew in my gut that serenity and a life free of suffering was a rational, reasonable goal. The question was not whether, but how?

. . . .

A lifetime of being in many ways two different people ... one strong with good self-esteem, one feeling embattled with low self-esteem ... sapped my energy. I often felt like the character in the comic strip "Lil Abner" who always had a black cloud hanging over his head. I certainly experienced moments of joy, and yet I rarely experienced happiness. The omnipresent cloud of self-doubt cast a pall on my spirit.

I was very aware that all the positive changes and experiences in my life had done nothing to alter the feelings I had been carrying with me in my gut ... at my core I still was consumed by insecurity, pain, and suffering. After years of lying to myself ... that I felt good about my life ... I was no longer willing to accept that status as being my fate. I wanted to be free of the pain I had endured for most of my life. I knew I needed to turn inward to find the answer.

While my SCA work had to a large extent freed me from my sex addict, that was just the relief of a symptom. The underlying problems remained.

I had no faith in psychoanalysis, having seen it fail several friends despite years of work. Besides, I already knew what the causative factors were ... no digging into a sealed-off past world was necessary. I had faced those facts, but that knowledge had provided no release.

Where then to find the path to the transformation I was seeking? Freeing myself would prove to be the most challenging task I had ever faced. Changing the habits and patterns of a lifetime, doing battle with my ego, would require much patience, discipline, and faith. It would not come easy.

2.

I found Buddhism in 1993 when I was 49 years old. As has occurred so often in my life, this positive development happened through a chance encounter. A friend who I had recently met through volunteer work at a gay social service organization in Chicago encouraged me to go to the local Korean Zen temple with him, which I did.

Upon entering the building, we were greeted by a smiling temple member who bowed in silent greeting to us. The zendo (meditation hall) in this temple is a very reflective, harmonious, formal space with a lovely multi-tiered teak alter on which sit a statue of the Buddha, various bodhisattvas, flowers and incense. Following the example of my friend, I sat down on a meditation cushion and sat silently, not knowing what to expect.

After sitting for 10 or 15 minutes, the resident monk sounded a small bell, at which the assembly stood up and began chanting something. I had no idea what they were chanting, or even in what language it was ... all I could do was follow along with the melody. (Later I found out that it was the three refuges chant in an ancient Korean/Chinese language that no longer exists.) Following the chanting, there was another meditation sitting followed by a dharma talk by the monk.

My initial reaction was, understandably, on the surface. The atmosphere in the temple was unique in my experience ... there was a sense of deep abiding peace, it felt like a refuge to me. This was very different from the experiences I had had either going to synagogue or to a variety of churches. (The great gothic cathedrals of Europe can feel like a refuge, but in those cases it's a function of the architecture, not what's happening inside the church.)

After a life in which my psyche had been in considerable turmoil and pain, the sense of peace and refuge I felt while sitting silently at temple (it would be a stretch to say I was meditating at that point) and listening to the monk's dharma talk was a welcome change. And somehow, the experience was not just a feel-good experience, but one where I felt there was something deeper going on. So I decided to learn more. I started going to temple regularly on Sunday mornings and after several weeks took an overnight Introduction to Meditation retreat that was taught by the resident monk.

For the next two years I continued attending temple every Sunday, giving my practice a communal base. And I meditated with some regularity at home. Typically I would do a walking meditation for about 10 minutes and then a sitting meditation for about 20 minutes.

After moving to Saugatuck, Michigan in 1995, I found a Vietnamese Zen temple in the countryside led by two wonderful nuns. Services here were just once a month, but temple was nevertheless an important supportive experience in many ways. Two experiences in particular during this time moved my practice forward.

After meditation and a dharma talk, the sangha would sit down to a Vietnamese lunch. Before we began eating, one of us would say the following Buddhist grace, which I took very much to heart as presenting a way of life for me both consistent with the positive aspects of the life I had led, and yet in important respects a new way of life with a new awareness:

> *This food is the gift of the whole universe -- the earth, the sky, and much hard work.*
> *May we live in a way that makes us worthy to receive it.*
> *May we transform our unskillful states of mind, especially our greed.*
> *May we take only foods that nourish us and prevent illness.*
> *We accept this food so that we may realize the path of practice.*

The first four mouthfuls
With the first taste, I promise to offer joy.
With the second taste, I promise to help relieve the suffering of others.
With the third taste, I promise to see others' joy as my own.
With the fourth taste, I promise to learn the way of non-attachment and equanimity.

And it was during my first few years at the Michigan temple that I fully committed myself to the Buddhist path and took the five Precepts ... the five moral vows or mindfulness trainings that laymen take, the practice of which is a core aspect of Buddhist meditation. As part of the ceremony, I was given the dharma name, Hanh Niêm, which means "Virtue of Mindfulness."

During the initial years of my practice sitting was a calming experience, but as is often the case for many people my mind was not quiet. It seemed as though my mind used the fact that I was sitting there peacefully to bring up every current issue in my life ... whether professional or personal.

The teaching is that when such thoughts come up, you are to simply observe them ... don't engage them, but don't try to shut them out, just let them flow through. Well, that's easier said than done.

I did find though that meditating on something I had read or even at times on a specific issue of the moment stopped the rapid random flow of thoughts and enabled me to bring the calmness of my sitting to a deeper understanding of aspects of the dharma or more clarity about the issues in my life. This wasn't meditation by the book, my mind wasn't quiet, I was engaged, but it was helpful.

The other problem, again very common, was maintaining my Buddhist practice throughout the day. Like many practitioners, I found that once I was off the cushion, my ego was back in charge and I went through the day reacting to things as though I had never meditated.

My experience of the first few years of practice thus made for a pleasant but not very challenging or deep exposure to Buddhism. The teaching I received at temple never pushed me far. And so, while my practice unquestionably gave me more periods of calm in my life, calm is not happiness. All my inner demons were still very much alive in my gut, and I was still a captive of my ego and its anger, fears, cravings, and frustrations.

It was towards the end of this period that I read a book that started to open the door to a deeper experience of Buddhism ... *The Tibetan Book of Living and Dying* by Sogyal Rinpoche.[4] As I read through the part of the book about living, the light bulbs kept popping in my mind.

When I read that, *"everything we see around us is seen as it is because we have been repeatedly solidifying our experience ... all our perceptions are illusory,"* I thought of all the problems and suffering I had experienced, possibly based on my own misguided perceptions.

When I read that, *"grasping is the source of all our problems ... so often we want happiness, but the way we pursue it brings only sorrow,"* I saw the pattern of much of my life.

Here was powerful teaching that resonated with me strongly. It was so relevant to what I had experienced in my life. I read the book several times, each time getting deeper and deeper into the teaching he was imparting.

This was my first systematic exposure to Buddhist thought and teaching. What a different way of looking at the world than the one I was used to. I learned that Buddhism teaches that our suffering (mental) is caused by our ego, not the things that happen to us; the problem is how we react to things. The layers of knowledge and experience that form our ego bury our true selves, our

---

[4] Sogyal Rinpoche, *The Tibetan Book of Living and Dying*, Harper Colllins, 1994

perfect Buddha nature that we were born with. If we were free of this ego, free of the known, we would see things differently and thus respond differently ... our suffering would cease.

While at this point I had just been exposed to these concepts ... I could understand them intellectually but certainly hadn't even begun to internalize them ... they nevertheless had a powerful impact on me and I knew this was the path to end my suffering. I looked at life and myself differently.

These teachings became my "bible" and provided me with the foundation for the deeper understanding of the Buddhist path I was to have later. These teachings gave me hope.

- *"Our true Buddha nature could be compared to the blue sky — clear and pure, open and gracious, infinite — while the confusion of the ordinary mind which we typically experience could be compared to a cloudy sky. The mental scurry of our thoughts and emotions (the clouds) obscure our true nature, but it is always there."*
- *"We must never forget that through our actions, words, and thoughts we have a choice. As the voice of your discriminating awareness grows stronger, you will start to distinguish between its truth and the various deceptions of the ego."*
- *"The noblest and wisest thing to do is to cherish others instead of cherishing yourself. This will bring healing to your heart, healing to your mind, and healing to your spirit. The only true serious goals in life are learning to love other people and acquiring knowledge."*

The experience of reading this book was game changing for me. It gave me the awareness that if I was going to progress on the path, I was going to have to go beyond the teaching I was receiving at temple and help myself.

Just as space explorers need to go to an orbiting platform before venturing into deep space, I felt I needed to create a platform of serenity upon which to build further explorations of my mind. For meditation to be transformative, I believed that not only is it important to create a physical atmosphere that is calm, it is important to have a psyche that, if not abidingly calm, at least is not in constant turmoil. Otherwise, try as I may to focus on my breathing during meditation, my mind would be bombarded with thoughts of the unfinished business of my life; my ego would not give me much rest.

And so I slowly built that platform based on the steps outlined in the following sections. It is a practical, realizable approach. It speaks to the goal of attaining a serenity that enables one to begin experiencing peace, happiness, and hope in the present by beginning to lift obstructions and frustration from your mind and soul ... a serenity that provides the peace necessary for the deeper exploration of your mind and the Buddha dharma.

I BELIEVE – THE IMPORTANCE OF FAITH

Because following the Buddhist path means going against the grain of almost everything in our learned experience, everything our ego and our culture tells us, I quickly found that it is not a walk in the park. It requires commitment, discipline and patience. And to be able to apply those three practices in the face of the obstacles and struggles we face daily requires deep faith ... faith in the teachings of the Buddha.

For many people, "faith" is a loaded word from their religious upbringing. But faith, or belief, in the Buddha dharma is qualitatively different from the faith that is sought in most religious contexts. Religious faith often requires belief in something that flies in the face of reason. Whether it's a belief in God, or belief in the virgin birth and resurrection of Jesus, or the Trinity, or the countless miracles ... all of these things require what's often called a "leap of faith" or sometimes "blind faith."

In Buddhism, the situation is different. In Buddhism there is no God; there is no creation story ... things just are. When most of us read a Buddhist text or listen to a good dharma talk, we respond by saying, "Of course, that makes such perfect sense. I can relate that so well to what I've experienced." In general, our intellect is on board rather quickly with our following the Buddhist path (with the exception of the few conundrums noted later in this book).

For Buddhists, it is the ego, our habit energy, that must be successfully countered if we are to make progress on the path. When the core of my ego screamed at me, "I want!" as I worked to be grateful for the wonderful things in my life or accept my life as it is now, it was only my deep faith in the teachings of the Buddha that provided me with the strength to say to my ego, "no."

That faith has two main components. The first is faith that the path provided by the Buddha dharma will end our suffering ... provided that we have the strength to follow it. That sounds like it should be simple. That is, after all, why we are Buddhists. Yes, there are many other features of Buddhism that make it attractive to us, but it is the desire to end our suffering that keeps us persevering.

And yet having deep faith in our chosen path is not simple. That is because at this stage of our practice we are still primarily creatures of the ego, of feelings, of perceptions; our true Buddha nature, our unborn mind is virtually a stranger to us. And the sum of our learned experience in the form of our ego will throw every thing it can at us to subvert us from the path. Only by staying focused on my faith in the teachings was I able to withstand this sometimes seemingly relentless pressure.

The other main component is faith in our own true Buddha nature. While this concept doesn't fly in the face of reason, it doesn't easily respond to the intellect either.

There are many rationale that compromise our belief in our true Buddha nature. One is, if we were born with our true Buddha nature and it's still there, why has it allowed us to suffer so? Why doesn't it show itself more clearly, even when we are searching for it? We often find this hard to grasp.

For those brought up in the Christian faith, another problem is the concept of original sin ... the exact opposite of the Buddhist belief. If you had the concept of being born a sinner drummed into your head in church during your formative years, it is understandable that the concept of being born perfect would be a challenging, albeit a welcomed, one.

Finally, because for most of us our true Buddha nature has been buried under the many layers of learned experience that form our ego, the fact that it is not visible to us, that we can't touch it somehow, is an obstacle to our belief. We have to take it as a matter of faith, until we are sufficiently aware that we begin to see glimpses of our true Buddha nature revealed to us. This happens when we begin observing without the intervention of thought[5] and we become aware of the discrepancy between what our ego is whispering in our ear about something and what our true Buddha nature is telling us.

Sometimes, visualization can be an important aid in understanding or projecting something. I had been trying for some time while meditating to somehow connect with my true Buddha nature, to visualize this non-physical thing, to no avail. Then one day, as I was meditating, I suddenly saw before me smiling, laughing images of me as a toddler. I knew immediately that there was my true Buddha nature, taking joy in the moment for no particular reason, full of love, an innocent in the world unburdened by learned experience. Not uncoincidently I'm sure, I had within the previous few months received from my mother both my baby book and an album of photos of me as a baby and toddler!

But at bottom, if we believe in the teachings of the Buddha, then we believe that each of us is born with our true Buddha nature intact and that it remains a part of us forever ... the one thing that is not impermanent and changeable.

Armed by our faith, there will be a counterforce within us whenever our ego tries to get us to give up the path or question it.

---

[5] As will be discussed later on, it is not that one doesn't have thoughts, but that one doesn't attach to them or engage them, and therefore they do not intervene in our observations.

AWARE BREATH = INSTANT SAMADHI

It's all fine and well being in a calm, peaceful state when one is meditating, sitting on ones cushion, but what happens while we're going through the rest of the day? Remaining in that state while encountering all the stressors of everyday life seemed an impossible challenge to me. Meditation became a time-bound refuge, not an every-moment lifestyle.

The usual advice regarding this problem is to be mindful throughout the day, to observe, to be aware. Unfortunately for most of us, mindfulness always seems to come after the event, after we have reacted to something in a decidedly unmindful way. This makes for a teachable moment, but does not help us much in the process of establishing a mindful state throughout the day.

The problem is one of focus. When we sit on our cushion to meditate, we learn from the outset to focus on our breathing ... breathing in, breathing out ... not to cut out what is happening around us or the thoughts that flow through our minds, but just to be aware of those things while focusing on our breath. This allows us to be mindful. But when we are not sitting, meditating, our minds are focused on all the various things happening around us.

One day while I was sitting, I practiced breathing in a way suggested by an article I had recently read ... I felt my breath come in as I expanded my diaphragm, rise up through my lungs, expand my upper back muscles, and then descend again to my diaphragm when I exhaled. As I practiced this method of breathing, and observed it, the image came to me that my breath was like a wave washing gently over my body. And just as waves cleanse the sand, so too my breath ... the breath of life ... was cleansing my body and soul.

I understood then that focusing on our breathing while meditating is not just a tool to help us stay focused; the awareness of breathing in and out is the basic building block of meditation. I realized that with each *aware* breath, regardless whether we are sitting on our cushion meditating or out and about, we are mindful, evils are extinguished, karma is purified, and obstructions dissolved.

But the question then became, how to achieve that awareness when I'm not sitting. When we sit to meditate, we are doing something purposeful that makes it easy ... well, easier ... to focus on our breathing. What we need to do, at least in the beginning, is to do something similarly purposeful at various points throughout the day.

The first step is to purposefully just stop whatever you're doing, mentally and physically, for a moment or a few. Because if you don't stop you can't take the next step and focus on your spirituality.

In Korean Zen, there are various chants/exercises based on the word, ma-um, which means, "mind." One of the exercises is, "breathing in we say 'ma,' which relaxes the body, breathing out we say 'um,' which relaxes the mind." This was something I could do periodically throughout the day, I thought.

And what I've found is that after doing the exercise (3 times in succession), I not only am aware of my breath, but I am instantly in the relaxed peaceful state that I experience when sitting on my cushion meditating. I may remain in that state, focused on my breathing, for as few as a few breaths or as long as several minutes, depending on what's going on around me.

Another technique that has worked for me is just saying the mantra, "Breathing in, I am aware that I am breathing in. Breathing out, I am aware that I am breathing out." Again, saying this 3 times in succession has brought me to a quiet, meditative state.

Once you are in a meditative state, and thus centered, observe whether you are or, more importantly, have been just prior to your entering this meditative state, in a state of equanimity, whether you feel compassion for yourself and others, whether you have been observing ... that is *not* engaging ... your feelings, whether you are accepting of yourself and the world around you.

If the answer to any of these queries is, "no," then if the situation allows, continue to meditate to regain the state of equanimity. If the situation does not allow continued meditation, at least you will be aware that you are not in a state of equanimity and be mindful of your actions and thoughts.

It may not sound like much, but these on-the-feet mini-meditations have enabled me to be more mindful throughout the day. Try it ... you'll like it.

THE SELF IN NO SELF

THE POWER OF SMILING MINDFULLY

Most of us are frustrated or at least concerned about many aspects of our lives, both large and small. So when we hear or read that the teaching of Buddhism says to accept things as being the way they are because it's just the way it is, we have a problem with that teaching. I certainly pushed back against it initially because I did not *want* to accept things as being the way they are ... even for a moment. I may have said, "I accept," but I didn't really accept.

On the one hand, I had approached Buddhism because I wanted to end my suffering, but on the other hand I really didn't want to do what I had to do to end that suffering. I feared the unknown ... if I accepted things as they are, then how would I pursue the rest of my life? (For more on this, see the section, "The Desire That Is Right Desire".)

While nothing can take the place of meditation in removing these obstructions and bringing us closer to acceptance, there is a shortcut to at least lessen the frustration and thereby ease that barrier ... smiling mindfully.

As you go through the day, try to be aware of your facial expression. If you're like me, you'll find that in general your facial muscles are either frowning or in a serious repose. This is our usual state when we're alone with our thoughts as opposed to being engaged in conversation with others or being entertained.

I regret that it was only after years of Buddhist practice and experiencing in general a state of peace and contentment that I became aware one day that most of the time my facial muscles were tense. And as I observed my tense facial muscles, I became aware that this tenseness created a state of non-joy that was at odds with the peace and contentment that I was otherwise experiencing.

Purposefully, I brought a smile to my face and found that this in turn brought an immediate uplift to my spirits.

Just releasing the facial tension made me feel lighter and filled with happiness. This is what Thich Nhat Hanh calls "mouth yoga." But I found that the smile and its impact were fleeting because it was mechanical and I was quickly distracted.

Then one day while meditating, I realized that if I were able to be aware every moment of the wonderful things in my life right then at each moment, without attaching, I would smile mindfully and naturally every moment. Even if I was focused on some concern of mine, I would at the same time be mindful of the things that brought joy to my life.

Well, every moment was perhaps too much to expect at the start. But every moment I was aware of my breath, I would say to myself, "I am grateful for all the wonderful things in my life right now at this moment," and as those things came to mind I could feel myself smiling. As time passed, I observed that my awareness of the good things in my life began to permeate my day and I smiled more, not just when I was aware of my breath.

But this experience raised a question in my mind ... if I was generally in a state of peace and contentment, then why was the default status of my face a frown or serious expression?

Generally we frown for various reasons ... our culture is so focused on wanting what we don't have (not necessarily something material) and on proving ourselves through competition, we are so attached to the past and obsessed with the future, and the problems of the world around us are so vexing that most of us are in an almost constant state of some degree of frustration or concern, whether consciously or not. If we are frustrated, we are not happy, and that agitation shows in our facial expression.

Was my frowning a sign of the deep underlying frustration and insecurity in my gut that my practice had not yet touched? Were the troubles of the world and especially

U.S. politics so overburdening? As a Buddhist I derive joy from the happiness of others, but the corollary is also true, I derive sadness from the pain of others.

Or was this default position merely a product of decades of negative muscle training brought about by my samsara-filled life?[6] I know from my baby photos and family anecdotes that before I was burdened by my ego and learned experience I always had a smile on my face. My father called me his "sunshine."

My hunch was "all of the above." Of course this practice of smiling mindfully did not change my underlying condition or the reality of the world with its problems. But it did provide me with a renewed focus on the positive in my life and increased my experience of joy and happiness.

The strengthening of this positive perspective brought me back to basics, opening me up to more fully accepting things as being the way they are, releasing obstructions, and going deep within myself in meditation. By doing so, it gave me more energy to tackle the challenges of life with Right view, free of illusion.

---

[6] Samsara is the endless cycle of suffering caused by our ego-driven unskillful actions and emotions/reactions.

TAKE JOY IN EACH MOMENT,
IN EVERYTHING YOU DO

A monk once said to me, "Take joy, Ron, in each moment, in everything you do."

In our culture, we are programmed to seek out things to do that will be fun. Whether it's going out and buying something, going to some cultural event, taking a trip, or countless other options. The point is, to do something other than what we are currently doing, something that is not required of us or part of our daily routine.

We always want something different, something new, to stimulate us. The result is that we take little or no joy in the everyday aspects of our lives. How sad when right before our eyes, every moment of every day, there is something to take joy in and value. It's all a matter of perspective.

For years I paid no attention to the monk's simple teaching and my life was very unsettled despite a disciplined practice of daily meditation and reading. Then one day while I was meditating, this teaching came to mind and I let it sit there while I observed it and took its measure. It was one of those "eureka" moments. I resolved from that day onward, at first purposefully, to do as the monk had taught.

To take joy in each moment, one must first be present in the moment. If your thinking about this and that ... what you're going to be doing later in the day, how some problem will resolve itself, whatever ... then you can't take joy in the moment because that requires the focus of being present. There's a time for those thoughts, but it's not when you're getting dressed or doing laundry; it's when you sit down purposefully to think about those things because you need to be present for those thoughts as well.

I remember that first day well. Purposefully, I was present in each moment, something that was surprisingly rare for me despite my years of practice and disciplined daily meditation; such is the power of our mind. Everything I did, from the most mundane tasks of washing and drying the dishes or feeling the soft material of a knit top as I pulled it on to more mentally challenging tasks such as reading to just looking out and seeing the wind play with the grasses, tossing their seed heads this way and that in an undulating ballet ... I literally took joy in every moment, in everything I did.

This practice is enhanced when you are able to experience, to observe what you do and the world around you directly, without the intervention of thought. When the negative labels are gone, you will, for example, be able to see the gray, rainy day for the wonderful, complex, interesting day that it is rather than a "gloomy" or "ugly" day. Even before you get to that point in your practice, just being aware of the labels and choosing to see what else is there makes a big difference.

Whether you live in the country or the city, are rich or poor, are educated or not, this practice is available to all. When you are doing a task, even a very repetitive or menial one, or just being you have a choice whether to be bored or take joy.

Be aware of the motions of your body or the actions of your mind in accomplishing that task and strive to do the best you can in accomplishing it. Do it purposefully, not carelessly; give it thought, give it structure, give it dignity. Be aware of the layers of texture and the countless minute miracles of nature or science that are involved in your being able to accomplish the task well or just in your being alive. No task is mindless; no moment is without wonder and dignity.

When you are out and about, whether walking down a crowded city street or walking through a country meadow, let all your senses be alive with the experience, free of thought. Let's say you're walking in the city. You have a choice whether to focus on the dirt and noise and traffic and find it depressing, or feel the energy, the diversity of people, the amazing fact that somehow all of this works in unison. Likewise if you're walking in the country on a very hot summer day, you have the choice to focus on how uncomfortable you feel because of the heat or you can focus on the hugely varied texture and miracle of nature that is available to your senses.

In a way, this practice can be thought of as a further step in the practice of smiling mindfully. When we begin that practice and think of the wonderful things in our life, we typically think of larger, more significant things that play a major role in our lives. In this practice, we realize that all the minutiae of our lives are full of wonder and available to take joy in; we are aware of the dignity of our lives. And being present provides the access, the door to experiencing that joy and dignity.

ACCEPTING OURSELVES – CULTIVATING A COMPASSIONATE HEART

For years I wandered through my life frustrated. It didn't matter whether I was doing something I enjoyed or whether I was keeping up with what was happening in the world. What I enjoyed awakened cravings that left me anxious and frustrated. What disturbed me in the world left me feeling angry and agitated. And of course not having what I wanted left me frustrated. The problem was that I was approaching everything in my life from a place that lacked equanimity.

If we want to be in this world and not be agitated by all the terrible things that are happening, if we want to do the things we enjoy and give our life purpose ... indeed, even follow the Five Precepts ... with equanimity, without awakening cravings and frustration, if we want to feel at peace and content, there is one clear answer ... acceptance.[7] Until I truly accepted myself and my life as it was right then and accepted the world as it was right then, I was constantly subject to the suffering, the agony, caused by craving, frustration, and anger.

The first step is to accept *ourselves* ... to have compassion for ourselves and love ourselves unconditionally. For myself, as for so many people, learning to love myself unconditionally and have compassion for myself was a real challenge.

Why is it so hard for us to have compassion for ourselves? One would think that compassion would be a significant coping mechanism. But our ego, while supportive of every manner of rationalization to justify our

---

[7] That is, this is the answer if one is not at the stage of practice where one has understood the illusory nature of all perceptions and the impermanence of all things, is free of your ego, and realized nonattachment. At that point acceptance is not an issue because there is nothing to accept; you and the world around you are one, free of labels, everything just is.

actions or our failure to act, does not allow us to feel compassion and unconditional love for ourselves because that would undermine the power of the learned labels that it ruthlessly applies to us.

"Wait," you say, "I have felt pity towards myself or sorrow at my condition." But pity and sorrow are not compassion, at least not in the Buddhist sense. Because pity and sorrow do not negate the underlying condition as perceived by our ego. It does not change the perception that we are bad or a failure or whatever.

"Well, what about all the people out there with huge egos? Are you saying they don't love themselves?" They may love themselves, but certainly not unconditionally and they don't have compassion for themselves. People with huge egos have been shown to be at bottom very insecure people. The huge ego is a façade that hides their insecurity.

For a Buddhist, the origin of compassion is love, whether for oneself or others. It is selfless and unconditional. When compassion flows from unconditional love, we do not judge ourselves anymore. We accept ourselves for what we are ... without labels.

So how do we cultivate unconditional love and compassion while still in the throes of our ego? The answer comes in two parts ... one organic, one intellectual.

Before we understand the illusory nature of all perceptions, before we have freed ourselves from the past and the future, before we are free of our ego, we come to believe in our own true Buddha nature ... that faith that I discussed in the first section of this chapter ... and we understand samsara.

We come to know early on in our practice that our samsara ... the particular combination of cravings and neuroses that we suffer from ... is the result of our learned experience. We become aware that our self-image is actually a reflection of the image others have had of us, not a reflection of unfiltered reality ... for example, we may not make much money or have much, but we are not a "failure;" we may be gay, but we're not "weird" or "sick;" we may be overweight, but we are not "fat;" we may have plain looks, but we're not "homely;" those are labels set by our culture, our peers, or our family. Even fear, guilt, and shame are learned as children. All our thoughts are molded by our learned experience.

And we come to an awareness of our, in a very basic sense, limited control over our lives when we may have thought we were quite in control of things. We are products of our environment and upbringing, and the way we are programmed by those factors limits in a very practical way the choices our mind can make.

At this stage of our practice, however, despite our intellectual awareness of these truths, we are not free of these feelings; we are not free of our ego. Our true Buddha nature is unknown to us.

But that awareness does allow us to challenge the thoughts we've had about ourselves through the organic process of affirmations. Affirmations are designed to displace our negative learned feelings and labels with positive ones that reflect our inner being, our true Buddha nature. Obviously the very fact that one needs to recite affirmations, at least in the beginning, indicates that part of you doesn't really believe them. In order not to get caught in that trap ... that is, affirming what you don't believe and thus perversely reinforcing that disbelief ... it is of critical importance that part of you *does* believe what you are affirming, whether it's your unconditional love for yourself or your true Buddha nature and that you acknowledge at least intellectually that all the thoughts you have about yourself are labels that reflect the judgment of family or culture, they do not reflect the real you. It is important that part of you can honestly say, "yes," to each of your affirmations and that you vocalize them with conviction.

In essence, what you are doing with affirmations is having an intervention with your ego. You are telling your ego, just as the Buddha might tell Mara, his spirit tempter, that you are going to pursue the path of peace and contentment and that you will not be deflected from this path with negative feelings. While doing this, always have compassion for your ego for it is part of you. The point is to empower yourself to follow the path you have chosen and that your heart knows is right by freeing yourself from your negative thoughts.[8]

Recognizing the power of my ego and the entrenched nature of these negative feelings, I began many years ago reciting affirmations. At first, I recited them while giving myself a bear-hug, which I found very powerful and cathartic. Later I began reciting affirmations together with other mantras each morning while doing my walking meditation prior to sitting.

Here are some examples of affirmations that either I have used or have given to others to use:

I, Ron, love, respect, and accept myself unconditionally.

YES, I love myself no matter what I do or have done, what I say or have said, what I possess, who I am with, whether I

---

[8] If for whatever reason you cannot yet even acknowledge these truths, then you are indeed in a rough spot. You have chosen to follow the Buddhist path to end your suffering, but you cannot end that suffering while holding on to your negative feelings. Every step forward will sooner rather than later be met with a step backward; you will have a few days of peace and then the ugly head of anger will rise up and assert itself. I know it's not that you *want* to hold on to these negative feelings, but their habit-energy has you captive.

If, like most of us, you are here, trying to follow the Buddhist path, because you responded positively to teaching that you read or heard, you need to reconnect with whatever moved you and meditate on finding faith in the teachings of the Buddha, which as stated earlier is critical to making progress on the path. Meditate on acknowledging the truths of samsara.

am alone, whether I am acknowledged or not, whether I work
— no matter what, I love and respect myself unconditionally
and have compassion for myself. I believe in my true Buddha
nature.

I, Ron, am a good person.

I, Ron, am loved, valued, and needed by others. My existence
makes a difference in this world.

My feelings of inadequacy or failure reflect cultural or family
judgments. They have no intrinsic existence; they are mere
labels that are a product of my mind.

My inner being is always at peace and happy even when
something happens to disturb me, just like the sun is always
shining and the sky is always blue even when it is cloudy.

I continue to recite affirmations and mantras to this day because ones practice needs to be disciplined. Even though my affirmations now do reflect my unequivocal, honest awareness about myself, one must be ever vigilant and aware that negative feelings may still occasionally arise even after years of practice, especially in a moment of weakness.

Another organic approach to cultivating unconditional love and compassion for oneself is to follow the instructions of Sogyal Rinpoche and first "unseal the spring of loving kindness" towards yourself and then practice "tonglen" on yourself ... the Tibetan practice of taking on the suffering and pain of others and giving them your happiness, well-being, and peace of mind. This process is described in some detail on pp.132-133. It is a very powerful tool I would recommend it be used in conjunction with affirmations.

Our awareness of the truths of samsara also opens the intellectual door to feeling compassion and respect for ourselves. For the first time in our lives, when our ego throws negative words at us ... bad, stupid, unattractive, failure ... we understand that these are words that reflect the judgment of family, peers, or our culture – they do not reflect the real us.

And although I am responsible for my life, at a deeper level I understood that until I broke out of the cycle of samsara by following the path, my ability to choose or reject and to see clearly was a limited one. Free will is in reality not free at all. Whatever we have done that we may feel remorse or regret for, those are things that often were not really within our control to do much otherwise. And so, we come to have the awareness that allows us to have compassion for ourselves, to love ourselves unconditionally.

But compassion does not stop with ourselves. We learn that just as all people are born with the true Buddha nature inside them, all mankind in every corner of the earth, regardless how poor or how rich, regardless whether kind or cruel, regardless whether civilized or not, suffers from samsara. The details may be different in different people, but the experience of samsara is universal.

The awareness of the oneness of all humanity in both its essential purity and its suffering opens the door to having compassion for all people. Even the Rwandan who wielded a machete or the Nazi SS guard who sent thousands to their death or the Charles Mansons of the world ... all of these individuals are deserving of compassion because they are victims of their own samsara. Regarding all one can truly say, "there but for the grace of God go I."[9]

Compassion and respect for all people ... and beyond that, for all sentient beings and the environment ... lies at the heart of Buddhism. It is the rock on which the Five

---

[9] Jesus' statement from the cross is also very relevant, "Father forgive them for they know not what they do."

Precepts rest. Every day when I prostrate myself, I invoke the Bodhisattva of Compassion with the Korean words, "Gwanseum bosal," and commit to cultivating a compassionate heart towards myself and all others.

ACCEPTING LIFE

How do we find acceptance for our life, when we've spent our life not accepting it? It's like the old question of the chicken and the egg ... which comes first? Here the question is, is one only able to truly accept ones life as being the way it is right now after realizing the impermanence of all things and the illusory nature of all perceptions, or is acceptance an important initial step that makes it easier to meditate on the truths of impermanence and illusion?

This is not a trivial theoretical question. The answer has significant practical implications for the practitioner.

We are all victims of our cravings, our unskillful desires. While in the grip of those cravings, it is very hard for most people to "wrap their heads" around the concept of the illusory nature of all perceptions. We think we know the world and our condition in it. To not trust our mind, our senses, is a very unsettling proposition. And so, I made little if any progress towards this very important marker on the Buddhist path. My samsara continued unabated.

Even when in the grip of cravings, however, we are still usually capable in calmer moments of being aware of the wonderful things in our life ... be it our family, our job, our hobbies, our friends, the wonders of nature, the warmth of our bed, things large and small, whatever. I don't mean to be glib, but regardless how dissatisfied one is with ones life, there are always aspects that give us joy or that we feel good about when we stop and think about it. That certainly was true for me.

Is there a way of using that awareness to make progress on the path to accepting life? I believe the answer is, yes.

The first step I took was to work with this revealed fact. I focused on the good things in my life without saying, "Yes, but I don't have ... . " I tried to be aware of those things and be grateful for them ... but not attach to them ... throughout the day, especially when I got up in the morning and when I went to bed at night. Writing a short mantra for myself on this subject helped me focus. This is the teaching contained in the previous sections on "Smiling Mindfully" and "Taking Joy in Each Moment."

When you have, if not turned your mind from your cravings, at least given the good things in your life equal time in your mind, then you are ready for the second step ... understanding the difference between skillful and unskillful desires.

One reason why we have a problem with acceptance is our fear of the unknown. "How will I pursue my life if I accept things as they are now?" Even if we understand that acceptance does not mean resignation, we think that acceptance entails letting go of our hopes and dreams. And the idea of that is unacceptable.

But that is not the case. As I discuss in the later section, "The Desire That Is Right Desire," following the path does not mean letting go of all desires and hopes ... just unskillful ones. What turns an otherwise skillful desire into an unskillful one is often its origin in a lack of equanimity. Your desire may be in keeping with the five Precepts and thus skillful, but if it is based on your running from what is, if you are dissatisfied, then it becomes unskillful; it becomes a craving.

And what causes this lack of equanimity? Why do these hopes and dreams seem so crucial to our being that they create the destructive cravings that bring us only pain and frustration?

Hopes and dreams may be a function of human nature, but the lack of equanimity that transforms them into powerful cravings that cause suffering is caused by something else ... a lack of acceptance of ourselves, of who we are, and a lack of acceptance of our lives. If we do not have compassion for ourselves and love ourselves *unconditionally*, if we want to be something or someone other, we will suffer. If we are so blinded by cravings that we cannot see that we have what we need, what is most important to us,[10] right now, we will suffer. If we do not accept our lives, we will suffer.

So, if following the guidance of the previous section you have accepted yourself, if you love yourself unconditionally and have compassion for yourself, then you are almost there; your equanimity has begun to blossom. To the extent that you truly accept your life as it is right now, your equanimity will be complete and your skillful desires will remain skillful; your cravings and frustration will cease. (I say "to the extent" because at this stage of your practice, it is likely that your deepest insecurities and neuroses will not be capable of being neutralized so easily.)

The other problem people face when contemplating acceptance is that that very statement brings up all the things about their lives or the world around them that they don't like. And so, getting drawn into those negative thoughts, they make no progress with acceptance.

Once again, one answer to this barrier is our understanding that all of our perceptions of our selves and the world around us are labels that we apply based on our learned experience. We may not have reached the point where we truly understand the illusory nature of all perceptions, but we do understand the concept of our labels. And just like the labels we apply to ourselves don't reflect the real us, our true Buddha nature, the labels we apply to the world around us don't reflect the real world

---

[10] And by "what we need" and "important" I mean whatever we experience at the moment that brings us well-being and joy, while realizing that all things are impermanent and not attaching to them. In other words, it's not the specific things we have at the moment, but the awareness that at any moment of any day of any year, there are things we experience that will bring us well-bring and joy ... whether they be things outside or inside of ourselves. Even in our darkest moments when our world may look very bleak, we know that those strengthening experiences are open to us if we are open to them.

either, even though those labels are strongly supported by our culture. When we meditate on that truth, the power of our negative thoughts, our dislikes, will decrease.[11]

Another answer to this barrier lies in the teaching, "it's just the way it is." Once many years ago, I asked a monk why, if we are all born essentially perfect, suffering was such a common human experience. His answer was, "It's just the way it is. It's like the law of thermodynamics."

When I heard his words it was like a huge burden was lifted from my shoulders. While acceptance was still key to achieving peace and serenity, that acceptance was made easier by understanding that things are the way they are because it's just the way they are ... even if something still did have a negative label in my mind. It wasn't really for me to accept; it just was. Similarly, the age-old question, "Why me?" misses the point ... it has nothing to do with "me."[12] Having absorbed the teaching of "it's just the way it is," it was easier for me to accept my life and the world around me.

Once I understood these things and that acceptance does not mean consigning myself to a life in the future that is devoid of hopes and desires, then I was able to take the third step, which is to *truly* accept ... happily ... my life as being the way it is right now. These concepts are synergistic. This is not a mental trick; it is an honest way of resolving a very real obstacle to making progress on the path.

The change this brought about in my life cannot be overstated. As an example, for most of my life, I did not love myself unconditionally or have compassion for myself.

---

[11] The point made in the previous section about what to do if you cannot acknowledge these truths applies here as well.
[12] This is not in conflict with the Buddha's teaching of cause and effect or the Four Noble Truths. The point here is that whether speaking of cosmic forces or personal ones, when you ask the larger question, "Why is this happening?" the answer is that it's just the way it is. There is no intelligent force or God that is orchestrating what happens.

And so I was obsessed with finding companionship, both for security and to feel wanted or loved. The perfectly healthy and skillful desire for friends or loved ones was transformed into a deep craving and frustration. My insecurity and anxiety were so extreme that even when I was in a relationship, I would be so afraid of losing it that my craving and frustration would continue unabated.

But once I began to love myself unconditionally and have compassion, and began to accept my life as it was, knowing that I could still have skillful hopes and dreams, my demons deflated and my desire for companionship returned to its skillful state. I know now that my fear of being alone was just a function of the negative view I had of myself based on learned experience. There is no fear of being alone when you love yourself unconditionally and are at one with all things.

But beware, the line separating skillful and unskillful desires is very thin. It is difficult to both accept oneself and ones life and desire what one does not have; that is why the two are usually thought to be mutually exclusive and all desire is classified as unskillful. Desires have a way of pulling one away from ones acceptance. In order to keep our desires skillful, we must thus be disciplined in the practice of gratitude and acceptance until they are so deeply engrained that they become a paradigm of our life.

One also needs to be aware that because our ego and its cravings are so strong and wily, it is quite possible that when one reads these sections and responds positively to accepting oneself and ones life as it is, that acceptance will be merely an illusion, a self-deception. In that case, nothing will have changed and your cravings will be as strong and destructive as before. That is why I italicized the word "truly" when I wrote, "to *truly* accept my life."

What one needs to do in order to not fall into this trap is to give your acceptance some space and time to take root. This is after all a major shift for us after spending most of our lives not accepting. And we need to recognize that our craving for things is basically an addiction ... we feel we need them to be happy ... and so we need to follow the practice of 12-step programs and commit to not entertaining any of our desires/cravings for a period of time ... however long it takes until you can honestly say that you accept yourself and your life as it is right now.

Your ego will certainly scream at you, "But I want [whatever]!" When it does that, you need to respond that you have what you need, what is important to you, right now and you have faith that if you live each day well ... living a life in keeping with the Precepts ... the future will take care of itself. End of story!

Having begun to free ourselves from the twin obstructions of dissatisfaction with our lives and craving what we don't have, we find that we are now able to practice the third Paramita ... patience ... and experience the abiding calm that comes with it.

As regards accepting the state of the world as it is right now, my compassion for all beings together with the teaching of "it's just the way it is" has altered the nature of my interaction with the news of the day and the world at large. No longer do I become angry and agitated. Instead I have concern and compassion.

As you focus on the wonderful things in your life and begin developing unconditional love and compassion for yourself and others, accepting your life as it is now, freeing yourself from unskillful desires, and practicing patience, then you will begin to experience the serenity and peace that is necessary to meditate on the twin truths of impermanence and the illusory nature of all perceptions. However long it may take to realize the emptiness of all five skandhas,[13] when you reach that state you will be open to surrendering your ego to your true Buddha nature and, as the Heart Sutra teaches, you will be at one with all things, experiencing things directly without the intervention of thought, thus ending doubt and suffering.

---

[13] The "five skandhas" are generally defined as the five physical and mental elements that comprise the existence of a person: form, feelings, perceptions, mental formations and consciousness. They are also referred to as "aggregates." The skandhas are discussed more fully and the definition tweaked and differentiated in Chapter 4.

STAYING GROUNDED

Once I achieved a platform of serenity, the challenge was then to maintain it. In addition to continuing doing the things that brought me serenity as part of a disciplined daily practice, there was one more necessary element ... staying grounded.

As I make my way through life, there were and will likely continue to be many challenges to my Buddhist practice and my serenity. I have found that this is especially true of anything that I put energy and effort into.

Until we reach a state of enlightenment, even if we have surrendered our ego to our true Buddha nature[14] and are in general at peace and content, feel at one with all things, are free of labels and attachments, and truly accept our life as it is, when we put effort into an activity, our ego often arises, looking to be stroked. And if it is not stroked, we get frustrated. (Of course if we haven't surrendered our ego, etc., the likelihood of our ego arising is almost a certainty.)

Even if your desires are Right desires in that they are of skillful origination and in keeping with the Precepts and your efforts are self-less, ego still seems to arise when we are investing ourselves in some activity and turns it into an unskillful one. Since putting forth effort is an integral part of living and indeed of Right effort, is there an answer to this conundrum?

Your initial reaction may be ... "Ah, this is a sign that I've been deceiving myself; I'm not truly accepting of my life or I'm not being truly self-less." While that may of course be true, it is not necessarily so.

It is an inherent part of human nature that when we put forth effort, we do it for a reason, for an end ... for example, to help others, to further our career, to resolve a

---

[14] For more on surrendering your ego, see the chapter, "The Last Barrier – Surrendering the Ego: The Missing Noble Truth."

problem, or just to learn or create something ... otherwise we would not put forth the effort to begin with. (NOTE: If you are doing such an activity because you feel the need to fix an inadequacy you feel, to "improve" yourself, then the activity is not skillful because it stems from a lack of equanimity that needs to be addressed.) And so, even if we truly accept our life, our ego often attaches unseen to such effort.

We learn that in pursuing a plan we should be present in the moment, not to attach, and not think about the future, about the outcome, but what if the present moment is a setback to our skillful effort? If we are not attached to our effort, we will say that it's just the way it is; the world will continue to move forward. It will not frustrate us. But if we have not been mindful and our ego arises and attaches to the effort, we will be frustrated.

For those efforts where, once we have produced something, we are dependent on others for its acceptance/use, a different dynamic often occurs. Rather than letting it go at that point, not thinking about the future, we often find ourselves consumed by doubt and desire during the seemingly eternal process of waiting for feedback and check our email or phone messages constantly for some word. This is very demoralizing and robs us of our peace. Without question, we have not been mindful and our ego has attached to the effort.

The solution to this inescapable conundrum is to stay grounded. Whether it's your job, your volunteer work, or a book you're trying to write or market, you must make sure that the task does not consume you and rob you of your peace.

How we stay grounded depends on how far along you are with your practice. If you are at the point where you have developed the practice of being mindful and of nonattachment, then the answer is simply to be mindful, to be aware when the ego arises, to not engage it, and to confirm your nonattachment to the activity.

But if you are not at that point in your practice, you can stay grounded by first being present, which will allow you to be aware of the things and people that bring you joy, know that you have what you need, what is important to you right now, and maintain your focus in life on those things, as well as being disciplined in your practice of acceptance, compassion, loving yourself unconditionally, and meditation.

The key is to see your frustration or anger as a red flag ... it is your canary in a mine ... that one of two things is happening: either you are engaged in an activity or pursuing a goal which is not healthy for you, not consistent with the Five Precepts, or the activity or goal is in the abstract a healthy, skillful one, but you are approaching it in an unhealthy way, for example it is a craving that stems from a lack of equanimity.

When you experience frustration or anger, the first thing you must do is stop. Without stopping you cannot apply your spirituality to the situation. Center yourself by watching your breathing, using a technique as suggested in previous section on aware breath.

To determine whether the activity is just an ego trip or otherwise unhealthy, first ask yourself whether the activity is consistent with the Five Precepts. If it is, then ask, "Could this effort realistically make a difference?" The more macro the effort, the more likely that the answer to this question may be a painful, no. If it is either inconsistent with the Five Precepts or just an extension of your ego, then you need to drop the project to regain your sense of peace and contentment.

But if your effort really could make a difference, whether in one person's life or many, but the problem is that you are approaching it from a lack of equanimity, then ... since the assumption here is that you have not yet reached the state of practice where you are able to practice nonattachment ... you need to find a way to approach the activity in a healthy, non-craving way.

For most types of efforts you will help yourself stay grounded by limiting your time exposure to the activity. Keep your commitment appropriate with your focus on the things that bring you joy, that give you strength, and thus limit any potential negative impact.

You can't do that with your job, of course. Especially in today's work environment when there is often pressure to work almost 24/7. But even here, you must not only carve out time for your family and other things that bring you joy ... those things must psychologically be the center of your life, not your work. It is a sad statement of our culture that for many people work has become their life; they live to work, not work to live.

A helpful compliment to maintaining the right focus in your life is to remember the teaching ... it's just the way it is ... and meditate on that truth. Whatever is bothering you about the effort you are making, it's just the way it is.

It's also helpful to remember that we have no control over the future and can have no idea what is going to transpire ... therefore why obsess about what will happen? It's a no-win situation that robs you of your peace in the present, which is where you really need it. Instead, have faith that if you live each day well, in keeping with the five Precepts, the future will take care of itself.

Another tool that helps keep things in perspective is to engage in activities that relax you, calm you (beyond the spiritual ones already noted in this chapter). As adults, most of us have a real deficit in this area. Even activities that we supposedly do to relax us, to get away from things ... like playing golf, playing an instrument, shopping, whatever ... do not relax us because our ego is involved in those activities. They may be a distraction, but they are not calming.

THE SELF IN NO SELF

What you need to do is some activity that puts you in touch with your inner child, that innocent being who was and is still free from the burdens of life and most learned experience. Most adults in our culture are closed off to their inner child; somehow it's not felt appropriate for adults to engage in childlike behavior or activities. And yet those activities, and the simple laughter that often accompanies them, give one access to the well of innocent joy that only a child experiences. Whether you used to love coloring books, climbing trees, playing with your dog (this is not to be confused with what adults do with their dogs in a dog park), or whatever, allow yourself the simple joy of immersing yourself in such activities with some regularity.

There is a deeper answer, however, to the question of how to stay grounded. There is a line in the classic Chinese poem, *Affirming Faith in Mind*, that says, "When the mind rests undisturbed then nothing in the world offends. And when no thing can give offense, then all obstructions cease to be."[15]

We are frustrated in these situations because our ego takes offense when we are not stroked. And the ego takes offense because these situations disturb our mind.

Why do these situations disturb our mind? Because we do not experience them free of labels, free of our past. For most of us these situations touch the deepest insecurities from our childhood about who we are, how we are valued, and whether we are liked or loved. Whenever we put ourselves, our talent, our credibility on the line, this ego insecurity is awakened.

And so the deeper, more fundamental, solution to such frustration is to meditate on the truth that fear, guilt, and shame are learned. We must free ourselves from the past. Whatever made us feel insecure as children, that emotional reaction was a learned experience and does not reflect who

---

[15] Roshi Phillip Kapleau, *Chants*, Rochester Zen Center, 1990

we really were; it was a cultural or family judgment. And those judgments do not speak the truth; they are biased. Our cultural obsession with "improving" ourselves is not founded on a desire to learn more or do other things, it is based on a perception that we are inadequate in some way, that we are failures, and that that needs to be fixed. But we are not inadequate; we are not failures. These perceptions of ours have no intrinsic value; they are all of dependent origination. (See the next chapter, "Coming To Understand The Fundamentals - Behind The Clouds The Sky Is Always Blue.")

And so, being free of these perceptions and feelings or at least aware of their nature, we meditate on being at one with ourselves, experiencing ourselves without the intervention of thought. And we meditate on loving ourselves unconditionally, finding peace and hope in the present..

As noted above, even if you are at the point in your practice where you've surrendered your ego to your true Buddha nature, this can still happen; the ego can still arise. "How can that be?" you may ask. The ego does not disappear; it does not vanish from our existence; it remains part of us. It may no longer factor into our view of the world and our everyday lives ... but when our innermost insecurities are touched it can arise and regain a foothold in our mind. That is why we must be mindful, be aware when the ego arises, and confirm our nonattachment.

Free At Last

> When I was a young man
> I was consumed by a silent anger
> Against the world and our culture.
> I felt unwanted and unloved,
> At times even despised, by others.

THE SELF IN NO SELF

I could not accept the world as being
Just the way it is
Because I felt unfairly rejected by the world.
Feeling rejected,
I perversely rejected myself,
Believing what I was taught by the world.
And rejecting myself
Enflamed my anger all the more.

But when I found the Buddha dharma
I learned that I and all others were born
Essentially perfect
With the true Buddha nature
That remains intact throughout our lives.
The things that I had learned about myself,
All the labels, were false.
When I understood that my perceptions of
Myself were a product of the world
And not a product of who I was,
I was freed of these perceptions,
I believed in my true Buddha nature.
And when I believed in my true Buddha nature
I was able to love myself unconditionally and
Have compassion for myself;
I was able to accept myself just as I was.
And when I accepted myself just as I was
I was able to accept the world as being
Just the way it is
And have compassion for all people.
And when I accepted the world as it is
And found compassion for all people
I was freed from anger.
I felt sorrow and concern,
But I was free at last.

Chapter 3
Coming To Understand the Fundamentals - Behind The Clouds the Sky Is Always Blue

1.

Illusion. All my life, my actions have been guided by what I saw, what I thought, what I felt. This is what made me who I am. As Descartes said, "I think, therefore I am." But in my study of Buddhism, I was told that everything I've perceived in my life, all my learned experience, everything that makes me me is illusion! And that understanding that fact is one of the essential keys to freeing me from my pain. Are my senses really to be doubted? And if I can't trust my senses, how then do I observe and act?

. . . .

Those initial years in Saugatuck seemed in many ways perfect ... exactly what I had been looking for, and more. I loved living in the country surrounded by nature and working in my garden. I had become active in the community and through those activities was not only professionally fulfilled, but I met some wonderful people who became my Saugatuck family. It was a rich mixture of satisfying activity.

Yet in many other ways, nothing had really changed ... or better put, I had not changed. I continued to feel quite alone much of the time ... most of my volunteer work was done in my home at my computer. Saugatuck was definitely a couples town, so although I had wonderful friends in town, I was generally on my own. I had no meaningful companionship, no special someone in my life to share things with, nor even a buddy to hang out with. And there continued to be ample instances that I saw as rejection

I had found great calm in my life through my Buddhist practice. And I felt intellectually that it was ok to be alone and coped quite well, only rarely acting out sexually. But my emotional problems were still entrenched in my mind and in my gut, although they were felt less acutely. In general, I just wasn't happy with my life.

I came to Buddhism, as do most Westerners, because I sought relief from the suffering I was experiencing. In our culture, people tend to blame their suffering on what happens around them or to them and thus feel it is beyond their control; they feel like victims. Often it comes down to being dissatisfied with what we have and not having what we want. I was certainly no exception.

Buddhism, however, teaches that our suffering is actually caused by how we react to external things; external factors are not causative, they are merely precipitators. This internal response in turn is primarily a function of our ego ... the sum of our experience learned from family, friends, and the larger society in which we live that shapes our perceptions. If we were free of this ego, we would respond differently and our suffering would cease.

Put another way, the basic problem as seen by Buddhism is that we do not know our true selves, our true Buddha nature. Instead, what we think of as our selves and our view of everything that occurs in our lives are formed by these layers of learned experience, the detritus of our lives. The result is that we are caught up in a world of illusory perceptions, a desire for permanence when all things are impermanent, a host of attachments and unskillful desires which cause us nothing but frustration and suffering, and an obsession with the future. We are unable to live simply in the here and now.

This all made sense, it resonated, and yet these concepts, which are so different from our learned experience, were difficult to really grasp and accept, let alone internalize, and so, I was never able to go beyond a basic feel-good experience of Buddhism. After six years of practice, I had not made much progress on the path. And the teaching I received hadn't been of much help.

Then a truly transformative person came into my life ... the monk, Huyen Te.

2.

In 2001, the nuns left the Vietnamese temple and in their place Huyen Te, a Vietnamese Zen monk, showed up one day with a group of followers. Huyen Te was like nothing we had seen or heard before. He had no use for ritual or for the etiquette of maintaining an atmosphere of peace and quiet in all parts of the temple building at all times. When we would arrive on Saturday mornings, it wouldn't be unusual to find Huyen Te and the other monks watching Power Rangers on television in the kitchen!

Most importantly, he had no use for teaching that did not go to the heart of Buddhist practice. He wanted to make those insights, that wisdom, available to all. Huyen Te knew that only through our understanding and ultimately internalizing the insights of Buddhism could we change the paradigms that control our lives and are the cause of our suffering.

And he knew that the path was difficult because it meant changing the way in which we viewed ourselves and the world around us. It required discipline. And so he started having meditation sittings and dharma talks every week.

The sittings pushed us beyond our level of comfort … with the nuns (and at most other temples), sitting was limited to 20-30 minutes at a time. Over the course of a few months, Huyen Te increased our sitting time to 1 hour 15 minutes. It was difficult and initially painful, but taking us out of our comfort zone and showing us what was possible was an integral part of his teaching.

The dharma talks were rigorous. Week after week, approaching the subject matter in different ways, he pounded home the two most essential truths of Buddhism … that our perceptions are illusory and that all things are impermanent and changeable. The latter is an easier concept to comprehend. But not to trust our eyes, not to trust our mind, the way we view things ... this runs counter to everything we know.

But after several months of rigorous teaching, I began to see clearly that these Buddhist truths were indeed a reflection of reality. Bottom line ... my feelings and perceptions, the labels I applied to the things I experienced every day, were a function of my learned experience, my ego, my internal filters. I saw, intellectually, that even my deepest self-defining truths ... my feelings of rejection, social undesirability, and being unloved ... were all illusory, not reality.

This new awareness started having a practical impact on the periphery of my life, on minor matters ... I saw things from a different perspective, outside of my ego. While this may not seem like a major advance on the path and my core suffering remained as before, I was very aware of these moments of clarity. Often this would happen while reading the newspaper ... I found that I reacted to events or information less emotionally, more objectively.

Why didn't this intellectual realization go further and impact my core issues? I mean, these ideas make perfect sense once you think about it. Yet our minds and egos – the product of a lifetime of learned experience and psychology – are so strong and cunning that understanding something intellectually does not at all mean that we will act on that understanding. How often have we all known that something was bad for us and yet we continued to do that very thing over and over and over again?

Constantly, I reminded myself of the importance of discipline and patience. If this sounds to the reader like a lot of hard work, it was. But then, don't most things that are worthwhile require considerable effort? For me as for most people the Buddhist path is an incremental one; there is no flash of instant enlightenment.

What follows is my take on the essential truths of impermanence and the illusory nature of all perceptions, as well as some further brief thoughts on how, now that we have hopefully built a platform of serenity, we can make further progress on the path from anger, craving, fear, and frustration to experiencing peace and contentment. By explaining these basic Buddhist concepts using metaphors of nature, using experiences we have all had, it has helped me and I hope it will help the reader dissolve some barriers. With the barriers broken, the path will be open to deeper understanding and eventually an end to suffering.

BEHIND THE CLOUDS THE SKY IS ALWAYS BLUE

We all know this is a fact. We've seen the blue sky through breaks in the clouds; we've been in planes that punch through dark clouds into a dazzling sunny blue sky.

The blue sky is a metaphor for our own true Buddha nature, the one thing that is not impermanent and changeable. Buddhism teaches that we are all born essentially perfect with the true Buddha nature inside us. That nature remains inside us throughout our lives.

The clouds are a metaphor for what keeps us from seeing our true nature.[16] The clouds are all the learned experiences that form our frame of reference to life and fuel our neuroses. Over the years, our true nature gets buried under layer upon layer of learned experience, which obscures our true nature from our view to the point that it is virtually unknown to us ... to the point that it is our ego that we identify with, not our true Buddha nature. It's like living through a long winter of gray days that never ends ... where there is no spring, no sunshine, no break in the clouds ... where it's easy to forget what the sun felt like.

The path of Buddhism enables us to see through this mass of learned experience and find our true Buddha nature again. Two of the most important teachings we encounter on the path are the illusory nature of all perceptions and the impermanence of all things.

The Illusory Nature of Perceptions

Think of almost any element of weather ... heat, cold, rain, snow. These are very objective, measurable facts. Yet one person will thrive in a particular weather condition

---

[16] For this metaphor, I am indebted to Sogyal Rinpoche's *The Tibetan Book of Living and Dying*, op. cit..

while another can't stand it. Our reactions to the weather are entirely subjective and change from person to person.

What causes these differing reactions? It's our learned experience. Whether it's the weather we grew up with, whether it's how our parents or peers reacted to the weather ... a variety of learned inputs form our individual response to the weather.

And this subjective view in turn causes many of us suffering. How often have we been in a weather situation that we didn't like ... whether high heat and humidity or unrelenting rain or snow ... which had the psychological impact of making us miserable and depressed?

What has happened is that our learned experience has caused us to put mental labels on everything that we experience ... labels that something is good or bad ... which interfere with our perception of the true quality of things. When a sensory image goes from the eyes, nose, or ears to the brain, it is these labels that impact how the images are received. Our conscious mind does not receive them neutrally.

The point here is that heat, rain, cold, snow, etc. are neither good nor bad ... they just are. Our perception of the "lousy" weather may seem very real to us, but it's all a function of our mind and thus illusory, not a reflection of reality. So it is with all things in life. We cannot know the true nature of things because the labels in our mind interfere with how we perceive all things.

For example, feelings of being inadequate or a failure, as well as all our various neuroses, are a function of how we view ourselves based on our learned experience ... whether that comes from family, friends, peers, or the larger culture. Hard as it may be to accept, such feelings are thus not a reflection of the reality of who we are; they are illusory perceptions.

To be clear, this assertion does not dispute the fact, for example, that we are unemployed, or making a certain amount of money, or tend to be introverted ... it disputes the label our mind places on that condition. And the fact that our culture supports that label makes it no less illusory; it makes it *seem* very real and makes it harder to free ourselves from that perception, but it is still just a creation of our mind based on our learned experience.

Let us take this a step further to the realm of ideas. I used to be a type "A" personality and believed that I was always right ... that my opinions were the right ones and anyone who disagreed with me was wrong.

Once I understood that all our perceptions are illusory, that meant that my view of all things in life was illusory ... caused by the various learned experiences I had had. Other people, however ... for example, someone on the other side of a discussion ... might come to a different view of things, a different opinion based on their learned experiences.

And so, while I still had opinions/thoughts (until one is further on the path and can observe and perceive without the intervention of thought, ones illusory perceptions are all one has to go by), I did not attach to them ... I did not label mine as right and others wrong. Rather I respected that most people come to their opinions honestly and that all opinions deserve respect. [17] From that point onward, discussions I had with people who had opposing views to my own had a very different dynamic and were much more productive.

But perhaps the most common and destructive illusion we all have in our culture is the thought or dream that we would be happier if only we had what we do not have. Yet

---

[17] I should note that in Buddhism there are things that are not morally consistent with the path – generally stated, harming others ... killing, stealing, sexual misconduct, and lying, for example. But one still has compassion towards people who conduct themselves in such a manner for they are but a product of their learned experience. For more, see the section, "Accepting Ourselves."

we know from our own experience and from psychological studies that attaining what we thought would make us happy doesn't do the trick ... at least not for more than a short period of time. And so unskillful desire is just another form of attachment to an illusion that causes us suffering by making us feel dissatisfied with our present, making us obsess about the future, and then causing us dissatisfaction all over again.

Looked at another way, the destructive force of this illusion is that it diverts us from being aware of all the wonderful things in our life right now at this moment and being grateful. And without that awareness, it is much more difficult if not impossible to accept ones life as being the way it is right now, without which otherwise skillful desires and hopes turn into unskillful desires and cravings. (See the section, "The Desire That Is Right Desire".)

With a general understanding that all perceptions are illusory, one slowly begins to release attachments and be more mindful, more aware during the day ... to experience things, to observe, directly without the intervention of thought, without labels. When thoughts do rise, we are more aware of this and of their illusory nature, and so we watch them rise and fall; we do not attach to them. And the more one experiences things with equal mind (for most of us this is not an all at once thing, it is incremental), the more our suffering and doubt cease. For during those moments, we see ourselves and the world around us unencumbered by ego and are at one with all things.

The Impermanence of All Things

"Will this never end?" "I want this to last forever!" How often have we raised that plaintive cry or made such fervent statements of hope? Yet if there is one thing that is certain in life, it is that all things are impermanent and changeable. It is a central tenet of Buddhist thought.

Here again, we have but to look at nature to see the truth of this fact. Nature is an endless cycle. Whether we look at the cycle of plants or the weather, the lesson is one of constant change and renewal. Plants bloom, go dormant or die, and throw off seed to perpetuate their kind. The endless series of gray cold days in winter give way to the sunny warmer days of spring and summer, which before long will grow shorter and colder as winter nears again. The waves breaking on the beach and disappearing become waves again through the cycle of the water's flow, the wind, and the tides.

No matter where we look, there is really no beginning or end, just an endless unbroken cycle. So it is also with human life ... all things are impermanent and changeable ... and while there is a physical beginning and end, the expression "dust to dust, ashes to ashes" expresses that here too the change is part of a larger endless cycle.

But we humans do not immerse ourselves in that wisdom. Instead, we attach to what is present in our lives at the moment or was in the past, whether it be something that we view as good or bad. And we obsess about the future. This causes us needless suffering.

In the first instance, we suffer when we have something we view as good ... whether it be someone we love, or a good job, or financial success ... but have an obsessive fear of losing what we have in the future. That creates anxiety and stress, which makes enjoying what we have in the moment almost impossible.

In the second instance, we suffer because we view something in our lives as bad and cannot imagine it ever changing because we attach to it. Similarly, although we may realize that some of our actions are destructive, there is often so much comfort in the known and so much fear of the unknown, that we still attach to the destructive behavior or situation and cause ourselves repeated suffering. Yet just when we've given up hope that something positive will happen in our lives, it happens. Despair turns to joy.

But the cycle repeats itself, as both the despair and joy are impermanent and changeable. Moreover they are yet another example of illusory perceptions caused by the mental labels that we attach to the things that we experience.

In both situations, if we were mindful of the impermanence of all things, if that was our expectation, then we would not obsess about loosing something we valued or continuing to be burdened with something that causes pain. We would just focus on the present, because that is all there is, and make the most of the present moment. "Nonsense," you say, "if I believed that and couldn't count on my marriage or any of the things I value lasting into the future, I would be a neurotic mess." But that's because you are trapped in the habit of seeking permanence. If you were freed of that habit energy, you would be at peace.

There is one fact of impermanent existence, however, that more than any other impacts how we live our lives … death. Each of us knows that at some point we will die … our lives will end. But most of us do not really accept that fact … we are typically in denial of our own mortality … and, in our culture at least, most have a fear of death.

After the death of my partner to AIDS, I certainly was no longer in denial of my own mortality; indeed, I was very aware of it. But I still had a fear, actually a greater fear, of death. And that fear made it impossible to be happy in the present because that fear fed my attachment to things present and future.

When instead I understood and accepted that I may die at any moment … perhaps tonight … and was ready for that eventuality free of fear because I understood the illusory nature of my perceptions of death[18], only then was I able to truly be present and take joy in each passing moment. Only then can we all be free of our attachment and obsession with the future.

Just Be

These human cycles I have described, which are caused by a failure to immerse ourselves in the wisdom of impermanence and illusory perceptions, are not like the cycles of nature and life. These are destructive cycles that cause never-ending suffering. The cycles of nature and life on the other hand are a source of freedom and peace.

When we know that all things are impermanent and changeable, when we know that all perceptions are illusory ... then we have come to understand the lack of intrinsic existence of all things, which is commonly but misleadingly, called "emptiness" (see the section, "The Fullness of Emptiness"). This is true both of the physical world and the world as experienced through our thoughts They are two parallel and interacting tracks of cause and effect, of dependent origination.

And when we live in that wisdom, have surrendered our ego to our true Buddha nature, and accept the fact that we may die at any moment and are ready, then there are no labels, there are no attachments, there are no aversions, there are no unskillful desires ... there are no obstructions to cloud our view, to lead us astray, to lead us down the dark paths that cause suffering.

Instead, when we reach that state of understanding, we are able to just be in the present, experience things without

---

[18] The physical pain I saw when my partner died was real, but my perception of death as a horrible wrenching event ... think of the common portrayal of death with his scythe ... was based on my not being able to separate the physical pain from my own suffering at his loss.

the intervention of thought, see things as they are, be at one with all sentient beings and inanimate things, and experience peace and happiness. We are free of all inner conflict and turmoil. We do not obsess about past, present, or future. We do not fear death. Nor do we run from what is. We live positive lives free of harmful actions and thoughts. We love ourselves unconditionally and have compassion for ourselves and others, free of fear, guilt, and shame. We are free of self.

Let me illustrate with a seemingly nonsensical statement: One can only find security when one realizes that there is no such thing as security. I have spoken about my obsession with the future, permanence, and happiness and the suffering that comes from the inevitable frustration caused by that obsessive search. Living in the wisdom of Buddhism, I came to understand that there is no security (as we think of it) because all things are impermanent and our perceptions illusory. Once I realized that, I was freed from the search for security. And once I was freed from the search for security, I was truly secure ... because I found peace and happiness in the present.

Regardless what befalls us, we are able to be at peace and just be. We understand the teaching, "It's just the way it is."

Now what I've been saying does not imply, as many people incorrectly assume, that the Buddhist path involves only inner growth and otherwise leads to stagnant lives. Buddhism does not imply nor require a rejection of or removal from the normal flow of professional and personal life. The planning for the future that is an essential part of functioning in ones career or job or ones personal relationships is consistent with Buddhist teaching.

The lesson of the Buddhist path is that by realizing the illusory nature of all perceptions and the impermanence and changeability of all things, we do not attach to our plans for the future, just as we do not attach to our opinions. Being free of such attachment, we are able to make plans or have opinions without the suffering that is present when there is attachment and obsession. One knows that whether or not the plans materialize, regardless whether our opinions win the day, the world and our lives will go on. We are aware of and grateful for our lives as they are.

Nor does a lack of attachment mean that one does not love ones spouse, children, or friends. It just means that one is not attached to that love.

Krishnamurti said that one cannot truly love someone unless one doesn't need that person, because only then can you truly know the other person. Otherwise, we love someone primarily for his or her ability to meet our needs; we are attached to that person. That is an illusory love.[19] But that is the love that is experienced by most, which is why there is so much divorce ... people grow and their needs change, and so their partners are no longer needed and not loved.

The clouds of our ego mind are thick and may seem impenetrable. But the path of Buddhism provides a rather clearly defined process that, when addressed with discipline, diligence, and patience, will lead to an end of our suffering and our experiencing peace, happiness, and contentment in the present.

Meditation – The Path

How does one travel the journey from the suffering caused by attachments, unskillful desires, and mental labels to a state of peace and happiness? How do we change the existing paradigm of our lives; how do we free ourselves?

A key part of the answer lies in the disciplined practice of meditation on a daily basis, building on the platform of serenity that you have attained. I am not going to go into

---

[19] J. Krishnamurti, *Freedom From the Known*, Harper Collins, 1968

the how-to's of meditation; there are plenty of books and articles regarding that. The essence, however, of all the methods is the same ... sitting with proper posture; being quiet and observing our breath going in and out of our body; being aware of our surroundings, but not engaging them; and observing our thoughts, but not engaging them[20]. Thus meditation is not about stopping, it is not withdrawing; when meditating one never ceases to be part of the flow of life.

Further, as has been noted earlier in this book and will be explored again later, we should not stop meditating when we get off the cushion. Instead, we should be aware of our breath and observe ourselves throughout the day (the reason for repeating this point is that it is of such a critical and difficult nature). That awareness or mindfulness helps us learn ... to see the cause of our suffering clearly, to see the discrepancy between our thoughts and reactions and what really is.

Note that I said that, "part of the answer lies in meditation." Before saying anything else, it is very important it realize what mediation can do and what it cannot. Many people get frustrated because they've been meditating for some time, as well as doing readings and other supportive things, and yet their suffering has not really lessened. They were looking to meditation to end their suffering, to solve their problems, and it hasn't. But that is not the function of meditation; that is a false expectation.

---

[20] As noted earlier I often violated this "rule" early in my practice for I think good cause and to good effect. I found that when my mind was being bombarded by thoughts, if I meditated on something I had read or even at times on a specific issue of the moment, that would stop the rapid random flow of thoughts and enable me to apply the calmness of my sitting to a deeper understanding of aspects of the dharma or more clarity about the issues in my life. This wasn't meditation by the book, my mind wasn't quiet, I was engaged, but it was helpful to my progress on the path.

What meditation does is provide the clarity to see yourself and the world around you free of the effects of your learned experience, free of your ego. It gives you ability to discern the discrepancy between what your ego is whispering in your ear and what your true Buddha nature is telling you.

It then is up to you to take this clarity and apply it to your daily life, to things both large and small, and thus to gradually free yourself from your suffering and ultimately surrender your ego to your true Buddha nature. (See Chapter 5, "The Last Barrier – Surrendering the Ego.")

Because making progress on the path is a struggle for most of is, it is helpful to find things that augment meditation, that help you stay focused on the path and not be waylaid by your ego. For example, to help me focus and create a new paradigm, I have been guiding my meditation by reciting the words below, as well as other mantras and affirmations, every day for more than 10 years. We may intellectually understand the new concepts quickly, but internalizing them, truly knowing them without thought, living them, is another matter.

Breathing in, I'm aware that all things are impermanent and changeable because it's just the way things are, and that all perceptions are illusory. Breathing out, I release all attachments and take joy in each passing moment, free of all frustration.

Breathing in, I'm aware of all the wonderful things in my life right now at this moment, am grateful, and accept my life as it is right now because it's just the way it is. Breathing out, I release all unskillful desires and am happy and content, free of all frustration.

Breathing in, I'm aware of the suffering caused by my ego. Breathing out, I choose to be free and surrender my ego to my true Buddha nature, thus freeing myself from the known, from my attachments, unskillful desires, and fear, thus ending my suffering and enabling me to take joy in each passing moment.

COMING TO UNDERSTAND THE FUNDAMENTALS

I am happy and content, at peace, in the moment and know that if I live each day well, the future will take care of itself.

Not only must we be disciplined in our practice if we are to progress on the path, but we must have patience and faith. Changing the paradigms that have been formed over a lifetime and which are inculcated by the prevailing society around us does not happen overnight. And it is made more difficult because our ego is our adversary in this effort, and it is strong. Make no mistake, our ego is not our friend in this effort ... it does not want the paradigms to change, it does not want us to be free of it.

But do not read this, or any of my other comments about the ego, and think I am saying that the ego is bad. It is not. It just is, as with all things. It is part of who we are and we should have compassion for our ego, just as we have compassion for our selves and others. And so following the path is not about getting rid of the ego, or putting it in a cage, it is about surrendering it to our true Buddha nature. My ego will always be part of me, just not active in my daily life.

Which raises an important point. Buddhism and meditation are not therapy. It is a path to see through the illusions of our mind, to connect to our true selves, and find peace and happiness. If we have serious psychological problems ... for example, if we suffer from depression or addiction ... Buddhism and meditation can play a very central role to ending that suffering, but it is not a replacement for therapy or a 12-step program. The stronger our problem, the more necessary it may be to use therapy as an adjunct to our Buddhist practice to help end our suffering.

The blue sky of our true Buddha nature is there, waiting for us to break through the clouds of our ego and experience the illuminating wisdom of our Buddha mind.

Chapter 4
Breaking Through the Dogma: Buddhist Heresies

1.

No self, emptiness, no right or wrong ... the iconic tag lines of Buddhism can be very confusing and frustrating. I am by nature a very analytical person. So when I read Buddhist tracts or listened to a dharma talk on these subjects, I was often struck either by what seemed to be internal inconsistencies or by things that just didn't make sense. And yet I had faith in the Buddha's teaching and had no doubt in my mind that everything he said makes absolute sense ... then, now, and forever. How to resolve these conundrums? What I'd learned to date hadn't helped.

....

Once Huyen Te got us to the point where we understood that all perceptions were illusory and that all things were impermanent and changeable, he started us slowly on the path to inner realization. He first told us to simply observe ... to go outside ourselves and observe what we see, observe what we do, what we think, how we act ... free of thought. This is to be mindful, to be awake. At first, there were brief moments where I was able to do this. But as time went on, there were more and more moments, and longer periods, where I was able to observe. And to the extent that thoughts still arose, my awareness that they were illusory enabled me to usually or at least often just observe them rise and fall.

Sometimes, there were occasions when I observed myself reacting in some habitual manner ... for example, getting flustered if someone who I had been communicating with on the internet was so rude as to suddenly just disappear on me ... and by observing what was happening I was able to stop, ask myself "why?", and change my habitual reaction. But when it came to the areas of my deepest suffering, either I could not stop my habitual behavior even when I was aware it was happening, or frequently I was not able even to be mindful in those moments and had no awareness.

As the months went by, my increasing ability to observe myself coupled with my deeper understanding of impermanence and illusion brought other changes in my relationship to myself and those around me.

For example, at one point I was heavily involved in efforts to protect the historic character of a local village through changes in the zoning ordinance. It was a very contentious issue and people's passions were aroused. One night after I had given a talk to a town meeting held to discuss the matter, one of the key opponents came up to me and said, "I will do anything I can to defeat this. I will lie, cheat ... anything!"

In the past, I would have fulminated against him and gotten very upset, both to his face and later, not just because of his incredible statement, but because I thought I was right and he was clearly wrong. Instead, I now respected that his opinion opposed what I and others were working towards. I just let him be, was quite saddened by the incident, and felt compassion for this man who was so filled with anger.

My deepened understanding of impermanence and the illusory nature of my perceptions also ended my previous obsession with finding security, as I mentioned previously. Freed from my attachment and from the search for security

I was truly secure ... for one can then find peace in the present.

This change in perspective had a very salutary impact on my sanity in dealing with relationships. My approach to dating was certainly very different from what it had been. I was able to be relaxed and present ... I was no longer guilty of "ordering the china" prematurely. I truly was no longer seeking, trying to fulfill a need.

This changed perspective also enabled me to weather a difficult experience with two long-term friends. Friends had been very important to me throughout my adult life ... I viewed them as a safe haven, loyal, and loving. Through my friends I received sustenance, felt wanted and liked. My concept of friendship was based on the relationship between my parents and their long-term friends, and like them I felt my friends were friends for life; I felt very secure in those friendships.

My deepened Buddhist practice was put to the acid test when suddenly over the course of a few months two of my close friends proceeded to dump me! One for a not well-articulated reason but having something to do with the fact that I had apparently offended his boyfriend, who was now going to be moving in with him, because we had not included him whenever we got together ... it was always just the two of us. Never mind that my friend never suggested that his boyfriend accompany us or even told me this person was indeed a boyfriend rather than just someone he was dating. The other wrote me a note, which was actually a nice thing to do rather than just ignore my phone calls, and told me that he felt that I had never really cared for him as a person, that he was just there for my convenience, and that didn't work for him anymore. And so with no hard feelings, he said goodbye.

To say that I was initially devastated is an understatement. These were both friends of 25 years! This sounds like a cliché but we had been through so much together ... we had seen good times and bad, laughed and cried, supported each other, shared our most intimate thoughts with each other. And now there was a wall of silence.

But at this point I was far enough along in my Buddhist practice that my reaction to this news was not a reinforcement of my old feelings of undesirability or rejection. I knew this had to do with problems they were having, not me. It just was something that happened, and for the most part I was able to accept it as that. It didn't make me feel insecure because I knew there was no such thing as security, except in the present. Now that was real progress!

2.

Through my meditation practice, the teaching I received at temple, the support of the sangha, and the little bit of reading that I did, my practice had come far in the last year or two, but some barriers to making further progress remained. Over the course of my years of practice, I had come across teachings that raised conundrums for me, as they had for other fellow sangha members.

If my true self is no self, than who am I? If what I observe is empty or void, does reality have no substance? How can there be no right or wrong? If desires are all unskillful, how to I make plans and progress in my personal and professional life? These conundrums went largely unanswered.

I had come far enough in my practice that the time was ripe for me to once again help myself. I needed to study the teachings and try to resolve these conundrums so that the barriers they placed to making further progress and fully integrating my Buddhist practice into my life would be penetrated.

The following sections, under the heading, "Buddhist Heresies," explain how I resolved these issues, not by finding an accommodation between Buddhism and Western culture to resolve the inherent dissonance, as has been suggested by some,[21] but by finding the answers in the Buddha dharma, carefully viewed, and having the conviction that belief in the Buddha dharma allows us to transcend our cultural grounding. Sometimes the problem was one of

---

[21] For example, in his otherwise excellent and helpful book, *Buddhist Practice on Western Ground*, Harvey Aronson does not accept that one must abandon various Western cultural markings in order to fully practice the Buddha dharma. He argues that one can have the best of both worlds. I would say as regards the issues he addresses ... self, love, anger, and attachment ... that the only answer is to free ourselves from our Western way of thinking and follow the Buddha dharma, properly viewed.

language, of how a concept has been translated, creating misunderstanding. Sometimes it was a function of much Buddhist teaching being stuck in a dogmatic rut. But the answer was always in the Buddha dharma. I had to look no further.

THE SELF IN NO SELF

A central tenet of Buddhist teaching is that there is no self, there is no "other," all is one. When one reaches enlightenment or stages in ones practice that approach it [22], one understands this oneness, this lack of self, and is free of ego. This allows one to experience things directly without the intervention of thought, without applying our learned experience.

No self also means being self-less in ones actions. Whatever we do ... whether it's our work, hobbies, volunteer work, charity giving, or working in the garden ... we do these things not to feed our ego, but to benefit others, whether it's our family, colleagues, the community, or the environment.

This teaching posed a problem for me, as it has for many Western practitioners. Does having no self, being at one with all things, mean ceasing to be an individual? As an example, I referred in the Preface to an article in *The New York Times Magazine* about a Z.en Buddhist master who had become disturbed by his inability to synthesize his Buddhist practice ... his no self ... with the continuing evidence of his individuality, his character, his psychological markings.[23]

This seeming conflict flows, I found, from a misunderstanding of this basic Buddhist teaching, taking the concept too literally or absolutely. One may perceive the intrinsic emptiness of all five skandhas and be at one with all things, free of ego, and in this sense have no self, and yet still have a self.

---

[22] In classic Buddhist teaching, there are four stages of enlightenment ... the stream-enterer, the once-returner, the non-returner, and the arahant, the last of which is referred to as fully enlightened. Each stage is defined by how many fetters ... the chains that cause samsara, such as self/ego, doubt, ill will, greed, lust ... one has abandoned

[23] See Preface

This is not an oxymoron. The self that is part of ones true Buddha nature is ones unborn spirit, ones elemental nature.

Proof of this can most easily be found by looking at the enlightened holy men we have encountered. Think of the Dalai Lama, Thich Nhat Hanh, and various other Buddhist masters. Despite their commonality and their oneness with all things, each of these enlightened ones have their own individuality ... their own elemental nature, their unborn spirit. They may have no self in the Buddhist sense, yet no one could confuse one with the other. They are not clones.[24]

When babies are born, they already have an individual spirit, a personality ... what behaviorists call temperament. And although much of what becomes of them will be determined by the environment in which they grow up ... the nurture factor, learned experience, ego ... their unborn spirit, the nature factor, as an aspect of their true Buddha nature, is unchanging. And so, regardless of the changes that occur in our lives, the one constant that remains throughout from birth to death is our elemental nature, our unborn spirit.

Do not confuse this elemental nature with ego. The statement that we retain our unborn spirit, even when enlightened, does not negate the teaching of no self. The doctrine of no self is about understanding the intrinsic emptiness of the five skandhas and being at one with all things, free of ego, experiencing things, observing, directly without the intervention of thought. Our elemental nature poses no conflict with this state of being because it is not a

---

[24] I am not aware of any Buddhist teaching directly on point. The concepts of the Five Buddha Families and Buddaghosa's Six Personality Temperaments, while describing energies that are present in both enlightened as well as unenlightened beings and thus somewhat related, really describe something different; those attributes are also thought to be fluid.

product of thought, it is not a product of learned experience, it does not inhibit mindfulness. It is innate; it is part of our true Buddha nature.

To those who would say, "No, what you call elemental nature is really what one normally calls personality ... you're just playing games with words." I would refer back to the empirical "proof" presented above. There is a distinctiveness to each of these enlightened holy men which cannot be gainsaid.

To those who would say, "No, what you call elemental nature becomes part of ones personality, which filters sensory experiences and thus does inhibit mindfulness and is not part of ones true Buddha nature," I would say it is not the elemental nature that filters, it is the ego that has attached itself to that nature ... just as personality is an outgrowth of that nature.

As our practice enables us to shed our ego and our learned experience, revealing our intact true Buddha nature, so too does it separate our ego and personality from our elemental nature, our unborn spirit. As stated in the classic Chinese poem, "Affirming Faith in Mind," by the Third Zen Patriarch,

> *When all is seen with "equal mind,"*
> *to our Self-nature we return.*[25]

Regardless whether one's elemental nature is one of sternness, seriousness, humor, joy, caution, or whatever, when one realizes the emptiness of all five skandhas and is free of ego, one can experience all things directly. Your nature will impact how you communicate with others; it will not impact what you observe.

To those who say that since the aggregates are the physical and mental elements that together constitute the

---

[25] Roshi Philip Kapleau, op. cit.

existence of a person they must by definition include ones elemental nature or spirit, I would respond that the essence of the aggregates is dependent origination. But our elemental nature is not a product of the mind, and as an inherent part of our true Buddha nature it is neither cause nor effect. Thus it is not part of the aggregates.

There are two further examples that show that a limited concept of self is consistent with Buddhist teaching. When we are taught to love ourselves unconditionally and have compassion for ourselves, that instruction makes no sense except with reference to some understanding of a self within us. Even more to the point for lay Buddhists is that pursuing a career or a relationship is not contrary to Buddhist teaching. Yet it is impossible to think of either a career or a relationship without some limited concept of self.

The key to reconciling these seemingly mutually exclusive concepts is once again to go past words to substance. The concept of no-self, of the oneness of all things, is about not being separate from the world around you, of applying no value labels or value judgments, of understanding that all sentient beings and inanimate things are in the boat of this world together, of surrendering ones ego, of being self-less in ones actions. There is nothing inherently irreconcilable between this perspective on the teaching of no-self and planning a career or thinking about a relationship or having compassion for oneself, even though these involve some concept of self.

Be on guard though, for this can easily be a slippery slope. If we think about our elemental nature or any of these real-life planning situations in a way that is not wholesome, either because it is not consistent with the Five Precepts or because the origination of our thought is a lack of equanimity or because we forget that every thought we have is empty of intrinsic existence, then we are indeed back in the control of our ego. The key to remaining wholesome as we go through our everyday lives is constant diligence and mindfulness. The trick is not to become attached to our thoughts or the things we do.

And what of our ego? What happens to it when one is enlightened or reaches a stage of practice that approaches that state? It does not disappear; it does not vanish from our existence; it remains part of us. But it no longer factors into our view of the world and our everyday lives ... except perhaps in a moment of great weakness when it is able to regain a foothold in our mind.

THE FULLNESS OF EMPTINESS

It is common in Buddhist teaching to say that all things are empty, or that they are void. To a person schooled in the English language, those words mean that there is nothing there. This formulation caused a significant barrier to my understanding and progress because I thought, "How can the monk say that the cup he's holding up doesn't exist? It makes no sense."

At first blush, this formulation may seem consistent with the related teaching that all perceptions are illusory. However, that is not the case. The point is that *perceptions* are illusory ... because our senses are first filtered through our thoughts and thus are a function of our learned experience, of dependent origination ... not that the things themselves, the objects of our perception, are non-existent.

Taking the cup example, when we see the object, our perception is illusory because when we look at it we apply labels seemingly without thought ... it's large or small, attractive or ugly. But the cup the monk is holding does physically exist.[26]

If a person cuts himself or has a late stage cancer, that person will experience pain, and that pain is real; it exists. However, when the person thinks about the pain, when thought creates fear, depression, or other feelings, those thoughts, those perceptions of the real pain are products of the mind; that is suffering. Another way of explaining this is to say that one cannot stop pain once the causal factor has occurred (short of taking drugs), but one can be free of feelings of fear or depression that our mind creates from that pain.

---

[26] There is of course another way in which our sense of the physical form is illusory because our senses themselves are limited. Our unaided eyes can only see the appearance of the outer form of the physical object; we are not able to see the actual physical structure of the cup, which is in reality very different from the smooth surface our eyes see.

The words "empty" and "void" therefore turn out to be bad choices in translating this central Buddhist concept. Recognizing this, much Buddhist teaching uses the phrase "empty of intrinsic existence." Whether one is speaking of the base skandhas/aggregates, or the aggregates as affected by clinging, they are empty of intrinsic existence; they are of dependent origination.[27]

On a personal level, the aggregates as affected by clinging form our mental and physical experience, they are the source of our identity ... appearance of form, feelings, perceptions, mental formations, and consciousness-ego.[28] They are a function of our learned experience, products of our mind. They have no existence independent of the mind.

Here again there is in the normal translation of the skandhas an element of confusion. The word used to translate the first skandha, whether base or clinging, typically is "form." Thus one says that "form" is empty of intrinsic existence. But the word "form" in English defines a physical reality ... whether it be our body together with its sense organs and nervous system, or the shape and structure of all objects ... and so form definitely has an existence independent of the mind.

Within the context of the clinging aggregates, however, it is our experience of form, the appearance of form, our delight or disgust with form, which is of dependent

---

[27] Throughout the discourses, the Buddha refers to both "aggregates" and "clinging aggregates." The difference is that the five aggregates just are ... if one doesn't attach to them they pose no problem. Even the Buddha states that he has feelings, perceptions and thoughts, but he doesn't attach to them and thus they do not impact him. Bhikkhu Nanamoli, *The Life of the Buddha*, BPS Pariyatti Editions, 1992, p.5

[28] The aggregates as affected by clinging are the source of identity and the source of our suffering. Bhikkhu Thanissaro, "Culavedalla Sutta: The Shorter Set of Questions-and-Answers" (MN 44), translated from the Pali. *Access to Insight*, 14 June 2010, http://www.accesstoinsight.org/tipitaka/mn/mn.044.than.html

origination and thus empty of intrinsic existence.[29] This is, in effect, the interaction of the other four skandhas with form, with the added factor of clinging. Thus my use of the phrase, "appearance of form," for the first skandha in this context to differentiate it from the physical form.[30]

Now, while form may exist independent of the mind, form, as with all things, is in the larger context empty of intrinsic existence as well in that it too is subject to dependent origination. Whether it's a blade of grass growing, or a rock in your garden, or oil in the ground, or the cup in our example ... all things are the effect of some cause, and as such they have no inherent existence. They are real, they exist, but they do not exist in a vacuum; they did not come to be independently of other factors.

How does one then experience the fullness of reality? The key is to experience things without the intervention of thought, and that in turn is only possible when one understands the emptiness of all five skandas, is free of ego, and thus is at one with all things. At that stage of practice ... obviously not an easy thing to come by (see the chapter, "The Last Barrier – Surrendering The Ego: The Missing Noble Truth") ... we are able to experience the sense world whole and complete, just as it is.[31]

---

[29] In reading the Khandha-Sumyatta, it is clear that the clinging aggregate commonly referred to as "form" is not the physical thing but our experience of form. For example, in SN 22.5, the origination of form et al is defined as "enjoyment of form, delight, and clinging." Likewise the cessation of form et al is defined as "to not enjoy, welcome, or delight in" form. Thus there is a distinction between the aggregate form itself and its origination ... derived from the four elements ... and the clinging aggregate form. Bhikkhu Thanissaro, "Samadhi Sutta," translated from the Pali, *Access to Insight*, 2010, http://www.accesstoinsight.org/tipitaka/sn/sn22/sn22.005.than.html

[30] Since the other skandhas are all mental in nature, I have not used a different phrase to differentiate between the base aggregate and that affected by clinging.

[31] As the Buddha instructs in the Bahiya Sutta, "when there is only the seen in reference to the seen, the heard in reference to the heard, the

THE SELF IN NO SELF

In the meantime, one can experience glimpses of that fullness when one is mindful and observes free of thought; remember this is an incremental process. At all other times, be mindful that our perceptions are illusory and that reality as we perceive it may be quite different from reality as it truly is.

---

cognized in reference to the cognized, there is no you in terms of that. This is the end of stress." Bhikkhu Thanissaro, "Bahiya Sutta: About Bahiya" (Ud 1.10), *Access to Insight*, 8 July 2010, http://www.accesstoinsight.org/tipitaka/kn/ud/ud.1.10.than.html

THE RIGHT WAY
WHEN THERE IS NO RIGHT OR WRONG:
ENGAGED BUDDHISM IS NOT AN OXYMORON

What does it mean in Buddhist teaching to view things with equal mind ... to say that there is no right or wrong, no gain or loss, no good or bad? Is one to take this literally? Are Buddhists therefore incapable of taking a position on issues? How do the five Precepts figure into this? And what about the "right" way of the Noble Eightfold Path? For years I asked myself how can one make sense of these seeming internal contradictions? The answer follows.

To have equal mind in Buddhism derives from being one with all things, experiencing things directly without the intervention of thought, which is to say without the interference of our ego, our learned experience. That's because right and wrong, good and bad, are all just opinions based on our learned experience; the labels we place on things have no intrinsic existence. Our ego thus is an obstruction that prevents our being able to experience things unencumbered as they truly are.

When one is enlightened, or reaches stages that approach enlightenment, we are free of the grip of ego, free of the learned experience of a lifetime. We realize that all five skandhas are empty of intrinsic existence. At this stage of Buddhist practice, we are thus able to experience things free of judgment, which is an exercise of the mind. We are free of confused illusions ... there is no thought of good or bad, right or wrong, gain or loss, and therefore there are no things that carry those labels.

But while we understand that our thought-based experience of the world is illusory, we also understand that it is not the case, as explained in the previous section, that the real world is void, despite the frequent use of that term in the translation of Buddhist teachings. It just cannot be grasped with power of mind.

THE SELF IN NO SELF

Where does that leave Buddhists then in making their way through the world? (And here it is important to note, as stated earlier, that the teaching of emptiness does not concern things such as planning how to grow your business, finance your retirement, or other such life matters; we are talking solely about the myriad of value judgments we make every day.) Do these teachings literally mean that there is no basis for supporting one thing over another, for taking any action of any kind?

The answer lies in understanding the difference between the thinking mind and the revealed mind. Let's take an example. Two people are disagreeing about something ... each of them applies their experience, their labels, to the matter at hand and come to different conclusions as to the value of the thing ... one thinks it is good, the other bad, and so of course they can come to no agreement. Both are adamant.

A typical person observing this interaction would apply his own perceptions, discuss the two choices, and come to a conclusion, either in agreement or not. A Buddhist who had reached the state of being free of his ego would, however, react differently. He would not view the issue as presenting a choice of one thing or another. There is a Buddhist poem that expresses the difference between thought-based choice and revealed "right" action with these words, "Not two, not three, straight ahead runs the way."

The reader may well ask, "What's this about 'right' action, when in Buddhism you say there is no right or wrong?" A very valid question.

In Buddhism, there are five Precepts which form the moral core of Buddhist practice ... not killing, helping others, refraining from sexual misconduct, speaking and listening with loving kindness, and not consuming things which are harmful. For individuals who are enlightened or free of ego, these Precepts are not external but come straight from their true Buddha nature. There is no thought involved, no analysis, no decision to be made ... it just is. For those who are not enlightened or have not reached that stage of their practice where they are free of ego, these precepts form an analytical tool to help them decide what action to take or not take.

But the use of the word "right" in translating this Buddhist concept is again misleading because "right" is a judgmental word. Rather, the word "right" in this context means "consistent with the Precepts."

The reader may say that this is still being judgmental. But saying that something harms another or helps another is not the same as placing a label of good or bad, or right or wrong on either the actor or the action. It's just a stated observed fact, albeit partly subjective.

Thus, free of ego and learned experience, free of the intervention of thought, with only his true Buddha nature to guide his actions, our Buddhist observer would say, "this is what one should do." Not because it is right and the other options wrong, or good v. bad, but because the course of action advocated causes no harm and/or is helpful to those in need.

The reader might well also say that having an action revealed as being right is even worse than making a decision that something is right because it brings with it a level of certitude which is dangerous.

Having experienced revealed justification for action from members of various religions, such as President George W. Bush, it is understandable that the reader would be very wary of this basis for action. Typically, people who feel that the path has been revealed to them by God seek to impose that path on others and will brook no contrary thought.

In this respect, there are major differences between the revealed truth of a Buddhist and the revealed truth of, for example, a Christian or Muslim. Buddhist revealed truth does not come from God ... indeed, in Buddhism, there is no God. There is only one's own true Buddha nature. And while Buddhists do advocate the path that has been revealed to them, they do so only by persuasion, with respect for the other person and his point of view, never by force of any type.

The Buddhist attitude is never, "I'm right and you're wrong," or "I'm Godly and you're not." Indeed, knowing full well the illusory nature of all perceptions, even the path shown by enlightenment will not be approached with the level of certitude evinced by others because there's always that possibility that one's enlightenment is also an illusion and so too then the revealed path.

This same awareness impacts those who are not enlightened, who are still to some extent governed by their ego, when they apply the teaching of the five Precepts in their daily lives. Knowing the illusory nature of all perceptions, having respect for others, and believing that most people come to their opinions honestly, even Buddhists at this stage of practice will not expound their opinion on a matter with the adamancy that one frequently observes in others.

Thus, Buddhists, regardless of the stage of their practice, are able to take action based on moral principles. Contrary to the understanding of some non-Buddhists, they do not shut themselves off from the world, saying in response to injustice and despair, "That is no concern of mine. Everything is the same; there is no right or wrong." Buddhists are engaged in the struggles of humankind.

THE DESIRE THAT IS RIGHT DESIRE

The Buddha taught that craving is one of the afflictions that cause us suffering. This thought has been touched on earlier in this book ... to crave what one does not have can be the result of illusory perceptions, a mistaken concept of permanence, and perhaps most importantly not accepting our lives as being the way they are now and were in the past. It has certainly been a major cause of my suffering. At the root of craving is desire.

The reader may have noticed that I have referred to such desires that become cravings as "unskillful desires," thereby implying that there is such a thing as a "skillful desire." Yet the concept of a skillful desire, a Right desire is not found in traditional Buddhist teaching. Typically, the two words ... desire and craving ... are equated, even though in Pali as in English, they are two separate words with different meanings.

Several years ago, however, I happened to hear a series of dharma talks on tape given by a learned student of the Buddha dharma on this very topic.[32] It made sense to me, it fit with the dharma, and I felt it was very helpful in making ones way along the path. And so, I want to share my understanding of that teaching with you.

As a Buddhist, the five Precepts ... not killing, helping others, refraining from sexual misconduct, speaking and listening with loving kindness, and not consuming things which are harmful ... are an essential element of ones meditation practice and form a core guidance on how to live a Right life. We know that vast numbers of people on this earth do not follow these precepts, and not only do they suffer for it, but those who they abuse suffer as well. Indeed, most of us can point to many moments in our own

---

[32] Larry Yang, San Francisco, CA.

past and even occasions in the present when we did not act in accordance with the Precepts.

Can one, as a Buddhist, "desire" to address this source of suffering, both by directly helping those in need and by spreading the Buddha dharma and bringing the benefits of its teaching to more people? Can we desire, for ourselves and others, a life that is in keeping with the Precepts? What about work ... can we not desire to help others through our work, in ways both large and small? In general, can we desire things that are consistent with the Five Precepts? Is this not what engaged Buddhism is about?

It was with much surprise that I recently found that the Buddha as well as Larry Yang would say, "yes." Listen to what the Buddha said:

> *What is right effort? Here a bhikkhu awakens desire for the non-arising of ... unwholesome states, the abandoning of arisen unwholesome states, the arising of wholesome states, and the perfecting of arisen wholesome states, for which he makes efforts, arouses energy, exerts his mind, and endeavors.*[33]

If that is not support for the concept of Right desire and engaged Buddhism, I don't know what is.

However, the teaching I received on skillful v unskillful desires notes one major caveat. And that caveat is that if such a desire has an unskillful origination either because of intent or lack of equanimity, then the desire is unskillful and a craving (or to use the Buddha's phrasing, an unwholesome state).

Let me give some examples. Desiring to help others is a skillful desire, but if that desire arises from the intent to create an image of oneself as being good, then the desire becomes unskillful. Indeed the unskillful intent in this case indicates that one is not really interested in helping others.

---

[33] Bhikkhu Nanamoli, op. cit., p.239

Desiring to have friends is a skillful desire, but if that desire arises from dissatisfaction with ones life as it is now, if one is running from what is ... from loneliness ... then the desire becomes unskillful; it arises from a lack of equanimity. Whereas, if one is content with ones life as it is now, accepts that it's just the way it is, and desires to have friends, then the desire is skillful.

Desiring to have a sexual relationship in a physically and psychologically healthy way is a skillful desire. But if that desire becomes obsessive, then the desire becomes unskillful because it arises from a lack of equanimity.

So, desires that are in furtherance of, or in keeping with, the five Precepts *and* are not tainted by unskillful origination are Right desires. They can and indeed should be acted upon for they move us along the path, they increase our happiness; they are skillful.

But beware that your ego does not play tricks on you. It is critically important to be mindful of the arising of desire and to be aware of its origination. To ensure that one's desires remain or become Right desires, it is essential that you *truly* accept your life as it is now. If our acceptance is self-deception, our desires will remain cravings. Thus, as explained more fully in the earlier section on "Acceptance," because the ego and cravings are so strong we need to give our acceptance an opportunity to take root before we engage in any desires, even potentially skillful ones.

There is yet one more caveat. As explained more fully in the earlier section, "Staying Grounded," the mere fact that you are putting effort and energy into something causes the ego to arise, looking to be stroked. This destroys your equanimity and the desire becomes unskillful.

To stay grounded and keep the desire skillful, we should both keep our primary focus on the people and/or things that bring us joy and meditate on loving ourselves unconditionally, acceptance, and the truth that "it's just the way it is."

Now someone might say that despite the fact that Bhikkhu Nanamoli translated Right Effort using the word "desire," such "good" desires are not desires at all ... a desire is something obsessive, it controls our life, it by definition causes suffering. Certainly most desires, wants, cravings fit that definition. But I would counter that a desire is simply wanting something that is not. So while the skillful desire I have defined is not harmful, it is nevertheless a desire. Indeed, if one is far along in ones practice and is free of ego, such a desire can result directly from ones true Buddha nature rather than be the result of a choice one makes.

Desire is not in and of itself a harmful thing. It is the nature of a specific desire and its origination that renders it a harmful craving rather than Right.

THE FOUR BASIC NEEDS
AND OUR DUTY TO ADDRESS THEM

We ... most of us ... are subject to the pulls of many perceived needs or unskillful desires. Because our needs and cravings typically relate to things that we don't have, the result is more or less constant frustration. And when we are able to satisfy any of these needs and desires, we find that we want or need more to "make us happy." The cycle continues and we never find happiness or peace and contentment.

Standard Buddhist teaching says that the problem is that we look to something outside ourselves to make us feel good, and that these cravings are, once again, based on illusory perceptions, which are products of our ego. When we come to understand that and are free of ego, we will be free of such needs and unskillful desires and experience joy and happiness free of frustration.

Even if one is not enlightened, ones illusory needs need not have such power. One just has to keep things in perspective and be aware that these are ego needs. What difference will that make? You will be more content, open to change and to non-attainment, and you will not feel frustrated (or at least not as much).[34]

While this teaching is central to helping us free ourselves from our unskillful desires, it is important to understand that it is not absolute. There are indeed four basic needs that are not a product of ego, but rather a natural part of being human. To discover these needs, we have but to look at our primordial selves in the form of newly born babies.

When a baby is born, it has not been subjected to learned experience and our culture. It has not developed a

---

[34] Of course, if one has truly accepted ones life and oneself, as discussed in the chapter on "Building A Platform of Serenity," then your desires will no longer awake needs and cravings; they will be skillful.

sense of self. Yet it clearly has needs as reflected in its crying. What are those needs? Food, freedom from pain, warmth/nurturing, and physical security. Those I suggest are the four irreducible basic needs of all humans.

But billions of people around the world do not have these needs met and as a result they experience pain ... not because they are caught up in the neuroses of their egos ... but because they are deprived of basic human needs. Even if they are Buddhist and have the awareness to understand that their lives are the way they are because it's just the way it is, are accepting, and have no unskillful desires regarding their state ... and even if they are at one with their true Buddha nature so that no circumstance will deprive them of their inner dignity ... they still suffer pain because pain is painful, hunger is painful, abuse and lack of physical security is painful.

Such pain is real, not illusory. Without any learned experience, without any labels, the first time an infant experiences the lack of any of these basic needs the sensation, without the intervention of thought, is one that by any other name still amounts to pain. Note that what is being referred to here is the sensation of pain ... physical or psychological, which is to be differentiated from thought regarding the pain which becomes suffering; the former is real, the latter is illusory.

Much of this experience of pain is due to poverty. Multitudes are so poor that they cannot secure sufficient food or, if farmers, their land is so barren that it does not produce enough; they are so poor that they do not have safe drinking water and live in unsanitary conditions and also have little access to medical care; they are so poor that physical security is a concept beyond comprehension; and financial difficulties increase cases of abuse and neglect.

Yet we live in a fantastically rich world. Even in this time of economic crisis, the elite in third world countries and the majority of people in developed countries are well off by any reasonable standard. They may be overstretched financially, but that's another matter.

Another frequent cause of such pain is being caught in the middle of armed conflict. Whether inflicted intentionally or as an unintentional by-product, those who conduct wars typically have a callous disregard for its impact on innocent people. What makes such situations more disturbing is that most armed conflict is senseless; it has no ethical basis but instead is a function of individual, ethnic, religious, or national ego.

Regardless of the immediate cause of these basic needs not being met ... whether it's a function of poverty, war, or just senseless individual violence or unmindful action/speech ... the underlying reason is a lack of compassion. Be it governments, corporations, peers, or even, sadly, members of ones immediate family, this lack of compassion results in action or inaction, which in turn results directly or indirectly in these needs not being met and people experiencing pain. The phrase "man's inhumanity to man" is not trite; it is a truism.

The answer to the problem is clear if difficult to imagine. The second Precept, as interpreted by Thich Nhat Hanh, says, "Aware of the suffering caused by exploitation, social injustice, stealing, and oppression, I am committed to cultivating loving kindness and learning ways to work for wellbeing of people, animals, plants, and minerals. I will practice generosity by sharing time, energy, and material resources with those who are in real need."[35]

But altruism has never been a strong suit of mankind, regardless of the culture or the century; there has been only limited peer pressure supporting it, even within a culture. While saying that, one must acknowledge that, as a result of progressive philosophies being adopted by governments

---

[35] Thich Nhat Hanh, *The Heart of the Buddha's Teaching*, Broadway Books, 1998, p.94

and peoples in the developed world, more has been done to help the disadvantaged in the last 100 years than at any time previously.

And yet, the positive actions taken by governments, religions, and individuals have been slight compared to the need and given the amount of wealth that has been accumulated. The excess of wealth and consumption in today's culture is obscene; and the rich (and by this, I don't just mean the super-rich) keep on becoming richer while the poor remain not just mired in poverty, but their basic human needs are left unmet especially in Third World countries. This amounts to a colossal failure of human beings, their governments, and their religions.

But the answer to the world's pain is not just material. The fourth Precept says, "Aware of the suffering caused by unmindful speech and the inability to listen to others, I am committed to cultivating loving speech and deep listening in order to bring joy and happiness to others and relieve others of their suffering." People, especially within families, often just don't think before they speak and certainly they often don't listen. This results in an environment that is not nurturing, conflict, and often, abuse.

To end pain on a large scale, we must start on a small scale ... action must begin with the individual. Every Buddhist, every person who considers himself a member of a religious faith, and every person who is an avowed secularist humanist should develop a sense of compassion towards all, commit themselves to the second and fourth Precepts and practice the golden rule, "Do unto others as you would wish them do unto you."

To strengthen their commitment, every person should instill this paradigm in their hearts and minds by reciting something like the following as part of their daily routine, be it meditation, prayer, or just getting started with the day.

Today is a new day, a new beginning.
I commit myself to doing onto others as I would wish them do onto me.
I shall act out of respect to myself, my fellow man, and my fellow creatures.
I forgive all those, including myself, who have caused hurt or harm to myself and others.
May I do whatever I can to lessen the pain in my family, my community, and the world.

The reader might ask, why should I act with respect towards people who are bad and do evil things? Why should I forgive those who have caused harm to myself and others?

The answer can be found in the old saying, "There but for good fortune go I." Every person is born with the true Buddha nature. But how they develop ... whether to become a positive, negative, or neutral force ... is a function of their learned experience and environment.

While society usually posits the concept of free will, it thus really doesn't exist, or better put, it exists within a quite narrow range of options. Seen in that light, how can one not have compassion for such people? This does not excuse their acts or relieve them of responsibility ... if one does harm, one must accept punishment; it just acknowledges that they too suffer from demons they cannot control.[36] This is in the same spirit as Jesus' statement, "Father forgive them for they know that what they do."[37]

---

[36] How this squares with a criminal justice system based on the concept of free will is beyond the scope of this writing. But for an extensive discussion of this subject see, David Eagleman, "The Brain on Trial," *The Atlantic*, July/August 2011

[37] Interestingly, in my brief research of this seemingly very relevant saying, all commentary seems to be on the asking for forgiveness. No one addresses the question, what did Jesus mean when he aaid, "for they know that what they do." Coming from a Buddhist perspective, the meaning seems clear.

The commitment to follow the second and fourth Precepts and practice the Golden Rule should begin within the family and expand outwards. No child should suffer abuse or neglect or not be shown love. Likewise, no spouse.

This point is so important it bears repeating ... no child should suffer abuse or neglect or not be shown love. Likewise, no spouse. If there were unconditional love and compassion in all families, if no child grew up feeling unloved or unvalued, what a different world this would be within a generation. With the greatest cause of neurosis and samsara a thing of the past, people would act with far greater equanimity and there would be less violence, less crime, less intolerance.

Is such change possible? Yes. People have their problems, their samsara, but one does not have to be enlightened to practice the Precepts and compassion. To fall back on ones own problems as an excuse is just that. What is needed is clear moral leadership from all quarters on this issue and lots of counseling.

From the family, compassion can then spread outward. If people within a community start acting with compassion towards each other and towards other communities of people, if that becomes the new standard of human behavior, then governments and even corporations will follow.

Man is a herd animal, responding to both leadership and peer pressure. Just as man can be lead to do acts of unspeakable violence and evil, or just acts of supreme indifference and self-absorption, so too can man be lead to do acts of compassion and love. What the world needs is a mass movement of compassion.

Chapter 5
The Last Barrier – Surrendering the Ego: The Missing Noble Truth

Ego. "Mirror, mirror, on the wall, who's the fairest one of all? Why me of course. Oh, you're saying I'm not so fair; I'm really pretty ugly?" The saying, "you are your own worst enemy," could not be more appropriately applied than to the Buddhist teaching on ego. But being aware that my ego is not my friend and, worse, is the cause of my suffering and the enemy of my search for peace and happiness hadn't diminished its power over me. Help!

. . . .

After many more months of teaching and practice, despite an increased understanding of impermanence and illusion and the nonattachment, clarity, and calmness that resulted, when it came to the core of my ego, the heart of my samsara, my suffering still had not ended. No matter what I did and had learned, I continued to bump up against an intransigent ego when my core neuroses were involved. What to do with my ego?

In traditional Buddhist teaching, the Four Noble Truths and the Eightfold Path describe the path to end individual suffering. The following is representative of how this teaching is often presented. The first Noble Truth is acknowledging the presence of suffering. The second is understanding the causes of suffering. The third is realizing that by refraining from doing the things that make us suffer, we can end our suffering. And the fourth is the path that leads to refraining from doing those things ... the Noble

Eightfold Path, which consists of Right View, Right Thinking, Right Speech, Right Action, Right Livelihood, Right Effort, Right Mindfulness, and Right Concentration.

Many teachers suggest putting this teaching into practice by mindfully ceasing to do the things that cause us suffering and doing positive things that bring us happiness. That's fine as far as it goes but the process is too circumscribed.

The catch is that in order to practice the Noble Eightfold Path one must first be free of ego ... the ultimate cause of all our suffering. One cannot practice Right View or Right anything ... becoming a stream-enterer ... if ones ego, ones learned experience, is still an active force in ones mind, because the ego will intervene by generating thoughts/obstructions which commandeer our mind and obscure our true Buddha nature, from which flows the various Right activities. Once again, freeing oneself from ones ego is central to making progress on the Buddhist path. Indeed, when one is free of ego, the gate to all Right activities is thrown open.

Actually, the Buddha's statement of the second and third noble truths goes more to the point. In the Discourse on Setting Rolling the Wheel of the Dhamma, the Buddha identifies "craving, which produces renewal of being" as being the cause of suffering and "the giving up, relinquishing, letting go of that craving" as being the truth of ending suffering. [38] To me, this is much more a description of the elemental force of the ego and the instruction that we must free ourselves from it than the lists one often is told to put together.

As the Buddha said at another point, "But to be rid of the conceit 'I am' – That is the greatest happiness of all."[39]

---

[38] Bhikkhu Nanamoli, op. cit., p.43

[39] ibid, p.34

But how to free ourselves from our ego? Many Buddhist teachers do not address this matter directly. Those that face the power of our ego head on, such as Sogyal Rinpoche, teach that as our discriminating awareness strengthens through meditation, we begin to distinguish clearly between the guidance of our true Buddha nature and our ego.[40] Eventually, the destructiveness of our ego will be clear and that will release us. Similarly, Krishnamurti calls for a "revolution of the psyche" and posits that understanding our conditioning/ego immediately without thought allows us to be free of that conditioning.[41]

Yet many have reached such realization and still remain bound by their egos; it is that powerful and wily. Recognizing the difficulty and the centrality of this action to leading a Right life and ending our suffering, the teaching that I received from Huyen Te (and later, Thai Tue), focused on a more defined path to free ourselves from our ego. I think of this teaching as the Missing Noble Truth and it is the core of what I call the Fourfold Path to Freedom:

Understanding that all things are impermanent and changeable.
Understanding the illusory/empty nature of all perceptions.
Practicing the Six Paramitas.
Surrendering our ego to our true Buddha nature.

Most of the teaching contained in this Fourfold Path is found in different Buddhist teachings: the Two Truths – relative and worldly; the Three Dharma Seals – impermanence, non-self, and nirvana; and the Three Doors of Liberation – emptiness, absence of labels, and just being.

Willfully choosing to surrender ones ego, however, as opposed to altering specific activities or thoughts, or being freed of the ego by understanding it's destructiveness, is not

---

[40] Sogyal Rinpoche, op. cit.
[41] J. Krishnamurti, op. cit.

a traditional Buddhist concept.[42] Interestingly, it is a core concept in 12—step recovery programs, which borrow many elements from Buddhist teaching.

By focusing on just a few key elements of traditional teaching and culminating with the choice to surrender ones ego, my teachers created a practical and powerful path to enable us to be free of our ego and thus practice the Noble Eightfold Path, ultimately freeing us from our suffering.

This path also bridges the gap or apparent inconsistency between the teachings of the Buddha on the noble path to end suffering, which are sometimes said to be for the unenlightened, and the teaching of the Heart Sutra, which says that when one dwells in prajna wisdom, there is "no creation of suffering or noble path to end suffering;" indeed, all phenomena are empty of intrinsic existence (see the following chapter). By teaching how to surrender our egos to our true Buddha nature, the Fourfold Path to Freedom enables the unenlightened to reach a step in which, while not yet fully enlightened, one is able to observe clearly the intrinsic emptiness of all things and follow the Noble Eightfold Path ... perhaps not 24/7 but many moments of many days.

The monks stressed that key to following the Fourfold Path to Freedom is the process of observing. As we went through our days, we were taught as noted before to observe both what we saw or heard, as well as what we were

---

[42] Although the Buddha's statement of the Third Noble Truth, noted earlier, appears consistent with the concept of willful surrender, other language in the dharma is more consistent with Sogyal Rinpoche's approach noted above. I think the concept is, however, closely related to the teachings of Zen Master Bankei on the Unborn. When Bankei would tell people that they were creatures of their partiality [ego] and that they should simply live in their unborn Buddha-mind, while the language was different, it was in essence the same as Huyen Te telling us to surrender our egos to our true Buddha nature. Norman Waddell, *The Unborn: The Life and Teachings of Zen Master Bankei*, North Point Press, 1984

doing, without the intervention of thought. For example, if I was driving through the countryside, instead of looking at the scenery and thinking how pretty it was, or what an interesting tree that was, running a mental commentary on it, I would just observe with no thought; if a thought arose, I would watch it arise and fall, I would not attach to it and engage it. Likewise, if I was in a conversation with someone, I would observe myself like a neutral third party. In these moments, it felt like I was disembodied ... like a separate part of me was observing free of my body.

In the early stages of this process, this ability to observe, to be mindful, happened only fleetingly and was often willed. But as time went on and my practice deepened further, the ability to observe expanded and became second nature, almost my default mode, till at some point I saw *most* things as they truly are, free of my illusory perceptions because I understood, not just intellectually but at my core, that these things are impermanent and changeable and that my perceptions of them are illusory.

Yet even with that understanding and my practice of the Six Paramitas ... generosity, virtuous conduct, patience/acceptance, enthusiastic effort and diligence, meditation, and wisdom ... when it came to the core of my ego, the heart of my samsara, my suffering did not end because my ego was still an active part of my life; I had chipped away at its edges, but that's all. I was not even able to be aware of such thoughts rising and just observe them rise and fall. My ego coexisted with my increased state of mindfulness.

And so, one day during a dharma talk, Huyen Te said that we had come far but we were still standing on the precipice. We were not able to jump because our ego was still in control and we feared an ego-free unknown. He said that the choice was ours ... having worked the first three steps of the Fourfold Path to Freedom, we had only to surrender our ego to our true Buddha nature. It was as straight forward as that.

This was true. I felt it in my gut. Yet even after years of practice, I could not take that step of surrendering my ego, jumping off the precipice. I acknowledged that the present paradigms that directed my life were to a large extent harmful and yet my fear of the unknown prevented me from taking that step.

And while I was familiar with the concept of surrendering ones ego from my 12-step work, and probably because of that familiarity, Huyen Te's suggestion that "that's all we had to do" was greeted by me with a resounding, "Ha!". It sounds so straightforward and simple, yet I knew it would be anything but.

But I had faith in Huyen Te's teaching and knew in my heart that the path he had shown us was the answer, and so after some procrastination and pushing back, I committed myself to that path. From my past experience, I knew that commitment and faith were key to making progress. I had to proceed with no more doubt or fear.

It is now many years since I first heard Huyen Te say we had but to surrender our ego to our true Buddha nature; that the choice was ours. After much practice and turning inward (see the following chapter), I did finally surrender my ego to my true Buddha nature, yet I cannot say that it never rears its head, that it has no influence. Enlightenment for most of us is an incremental path; indeed, if I ever reach that state, I do not know how I would know it. But I am observing now through different eyes and when it whispers in my ear, I am fully aware and mindful. My suffering has ceased.

Chapter 6
Finding Peace, If Not Enlightenment, and The Lessons of the Heart Sutra

1.

Freedom from the known. As the Buddha said, "But to be rid of the conceit 'I am' – that is the greatest happiness of all." I thought I knew so much and had come so far, but that was part of the problem. It was only when I humbly went back to basics that I reconnected with the light of my true Buddha mind and discovered my oneness with all things.

. . . .

Over the course of the next four years my practice continued to deepen, supported by my experiences at the temple, not just from the teaching I received but by the good fellowship of the other members of the sangha. In Buddhism one takes refuge in the three jewels ... the Buddha, the Dharma, and the Sangha. Without question, the warmth and community that was our sangha was a wonderful weekly experience for me.

After about two years, Huyen Te left to roam the country, teaching elsewhere, and a fellow Vietnamese monk, Thai Tue, took his place. His methods were different, but the teaching was the same. It is truly remarkable to me that in western Michigan, in the middle of nowhere (Bradley, the "town" where the temple is located, is little more than a crossroads in the middle of the countryside), I was able during the years I lived in Saugatuck to obtain such profound Buddhist teaching.

Years later, when I read that Zen Master Bankei had described some teaching as "scratching an itchy foot with my shoe on. It's not getting to the itch. The teachings don't strike home to the center, to the real marrow,"[43] I knew precisely what he meant. And that in Huyen Te and Thai Tue I had found teachers that did indeed get to the marrow.

Two things happened during this period of time that were significant in moving me along my path and further loosening the chains of the past.

I had been trying for some time while meditating to somehow connect with my true Buddha nature, to visualize this non-physical thing, to no avail. Then one day as I was meditating I suddenly saw before me smiling, laughing images of me as a young toddler. I knew immediately that there was my true Buddha nature, taking joy in the moment for no particular reason, full of love, an innocent in the world unburdened by learned experience ... and I cried deeply and long. Not uncoincidently I'm sure, my mother had within the previous few months sent me both my baby book and an album of photos of me as a baby and toddler!

Then one day, a year or so after that, while in the process of going through my files to clean them out, I came upon two letters from my father that I had totally forgotten about. One was a letter he wrote to me in 1985 on my 41st birthday. In it he said, "*I look at the pictures which surround me in my room, and memories appear on the original video screen of the brain: What a sunshine you always were. Even in your misery [I had terrible sinus and poison ivy problems] you remained gentle and lovable.*"

The other was a copy of a letter that my father had written in 1956 just before he was to undergo an operation, and which my mother had sent me in 1993, four years after

---

[43] Norman Waddell, op. cit., p.52

his death. Although the operation was not a hazardous one, he wrote the letter just in case things went badly and he did not survive. In the letter he said, "*I am proud of you boys, knowing that you have all the things in you that will make you an asset to society and men to be loved by your family and friends. ... Thanks for all the joy and happiness you brought into my life.*"

In the letter he went on to write about himself, "*I want you to remember me as the husband and father who had the strength and the courage to tackle all the problems of life and who loved his independence and his privilege to live as a free man more than anything else, excepting his family. A man who loved everything ... his work, his duties, his friends, animals, nature, people in general, and who always tried to see the good in everybody and everything. I will watch you from the distance and you will fill my heart with joy if you live a positive life, going ahead and doing things which are good and keeping up the high spiritual and ethical standard of our family.*"

After reading these letters, I broke down and sobbed uncontrollably for some time. Here was tangible proof of the love that I had always sought to be reassured of. And I realized that I had been so wound up in my hurt and the perception of not being loved, so committed to distancing myself emotionally from my father through all those years, that when I had originally received those two letters they did not make a dent in that perception, and the letters went unremembered until I went through my files that day. I had been that closed to his love. What a loss.

I had always been aware of the profound positive impact that my father had had on my character, but that awareness and gratitude didn't translate into deep warmth and affection; it didn't cross the barrier I had erected. Now, reading here his eloquent expression of who he was as a person, what he believed in, what he wanted in life ... together with his expressions of love for me ... I was overwhelmed with feelings of love and, again, loss.

2.

Over the years, one of the most compelling chants I recited at temple was the Heart Sutra. If you are not yet familiar with it, it is, with its contemplation on emptiness and the process of spiritual development that leads to enlightenment, a central sutra of the Buddhist Mahayana tradition. Its core truths are the key to freeing ourselves and it is typically chanted on a regular basis.

But after years of chanting the sutra in various translations, I had the feeling as my practice deepened that the translations were inadequate. Some suffered from a use of English that lacked clarity or just seemed wrong. And all seemed to me to be missing something important in the first verse.

In that verse, these versions uniformly stated that when the Bodhisattva Avelokiteshvara perceived that all five skandhas were empty of intrinsic existence his suffering ceased. The causal connection is direct. So, for example, in the lovely translation by Roshi Philip Kapleau:

"saw the emptiness of all five skandhas and sundered the bonds that create suffering."[44]

It seemed to me that as a teaching tool, which the sutras are, the concept of the oneness of all things, of experiencing things without the intervention of thought, was missing as a bridge from realizing the emptiness of the skandhas to being free of suffering. I know how presumptuous this must sound, but I felt it in my gut.

Having been a onetime student of language, I knew the problems and misunderstandings that can result depending on how words are translated. After not being able to find a

---

[44]Roshi Philip Kapleau, op. cit.

monk who was interested in working on this project with me, I decided to give it a go myself.

I chose to base my translation on the Chinese text and so gathered several Chinese editions of the sutra. In comparing them, I found that they all were identical and so felt safe proceeding with the project. Armed with several Chinese dictionaries I tackled the translation.

As I worked through the first verse, I found what I had thought had to be there. Between the phrase positing the perception of the emptiness of the skandhas and that regarding the cessation of suffering was the phrase "度一", literally "passing through one." Taking the liberties in translation (and exposition) that are not uncommon in these texts to clarify meaning, I translated this phrase:

> *"Thus being at one with all things,*
> *Experiencing things directly without the intervention of thought"*

What follows is my translation of the Heart Sutra.[45]

---

[45] I should note that in the process of working on this project, I found that in the Sanskrit text, and the Tibetan text derived from the Sanskrit, the first verse ends with perceiving the emptiness of the skandhas; there is no mention of suffering ceasing. The Chinese translation dates from around 400 A.D. and was done by a well-known Indian scholar and Buddhist missionary. I have found no explanation for this apparent variance. Since the Heart Sutra is not a sutra that was delivered by the Buddha, it would seem that one could use either version, depending on ones Buddhist lineage.

Prajna Paramita Hridaya – Heart of Perfected Wisdom

The Bodhisattva Avelokiteshvara,
Practicing the perfection of wisdom, going deep within,
Was illuminated and perceived that
All five skandhas are empty of intrinsic existence.
Thus being at one with all things,
Experiencing things directly without the intervention of
    thought,
All suffering and doubt ceased.

Shariputra, the appearance of form is not separate from
    emptiness,
Emptiness is not separate from the appearance of form,
The appearance of form is one with emptiness,
Emptiness is one with appearance of form.
The same is true for feelings, perceptions, mental
    formations, and consciousness-ego.

Shariputra, all dharmas – all appearance of phenomena – are
    mutually empty:
There is neither birth nor death,
Neither defilement nor purity,
Neither gain nor loss.

Therefore, within emptiness there is no appearance of form
No feelings, perceptions, mental formations, or
    consciousness-ego,
No eye, ear, nose, tongue, body, thought,
No color, sound, smell, taste, touch, or the appearance of
    phenomena,
Not even the domain of sight
Nor the domain of consciousness-ego.

THE SELF IN NO SELF

No ignorance or end of ignorance,
Nor aging and death or end of them,
No creation of suffering or noble path to end suffering.
No wisdom nor its attainment,
There is nothing to attain.

Bodhisattvas, abiding always in perfected wisdom,
Their minds have no fears or obstructions,
Therefore they have no fears or obstructions;
Free of confused illusions,
They reach nirvana.

All Buddhas of past, present, and future time,
Abiding always in perfected wisdom
Come to full enlightenment.

Therefore let all know that perfected wisdom
Is the most spiritual mantra,
The most radiant mantra.
None is higher than it
Nor equal to it,
It is able to relieve all suffering,
It is the essence of truth, not false.

Therefore, say the mantra of perfected wisdom:
Gate gate,
Paragate,
Parasamgate,
Bodhi svaha

For me, the power of this sutra is that it does not describe what it is like to be enlightened, but rather it shows the path, or markers on the path, to enlightenment. Boddhisatvas after all are not yet enlightened beings ... the Buddha himself referred to his pre-enlightened state as a Boddhisatva.[46]

There are several sections of the sutra that are especially edifying and became more so for me through my translation work. The first verse states in just a few scant words the essence of Buddhist teaching ... that all our perceptions are illusory, without inherent existence, and that when we realize this we are able to be one with all things (having surrendered our ego to our true Buddha nature). All barriers are gone, and we experience and observe things without the intervention of thought.[47] It is this freedom from thought that ends our doubt and suffering.

As a later verse reiterates, when you reach this state "your mind has no fears or obstructions, therefore you have no fears or obstructions. Free of confused illusions, you reach nirvana." You have freed yourself from the known.

The point is that our lives are ruled by the labels our learned experience places on everything we encounter in life and that when one reaches the stage of ones practice that is the perfection of wisdom, one is free of these labels and their resulting obstructions.

The verses that list examples of this truth are powerful indeed. "There is neither birth nor death." This seemingly clear statement gives many people pause at first. But the sutra here does not contradict this central fact of life or the Buddha's teaching ... that all things that arise eventually fall ... rather it means that our thoughts about birth and death, our perception of those two states, are illusory. And when

---

[46] B. Nanamoli, op. cit., p.10
[47] Again to be clear. as noted in an earlier footnote, thought and the aggregates are always present, even the Buddha had feelings, perceptions, and thoughts, but by not attaching to our thoughts, they do not intervene in our experience of things.

we realize that the five skandhas are empty of intrinsic existence, those perceptions fall away. The labels, the way we think of birth and death are no more. And so the fear we have of death based on those labels is no more.

The same is true of "neither defilement or purity." Many people reading the sutra for the first time again just shake their heads in bewilderment. "How can there be no such thing as defilement?"

But here too, the sutra is not saying that the acts that we label as defilement don't happen ... bad things happen to many innocent people ... but that the interpretation of these acts as a defilement of the person have no intrinsic nature. One is defiled only because our culture or learned experience says you are defiled. Whereas if you know that your true Buddha nature is totally unaffected by what has happened, then you are not defiled and the experience of the act does not cause mental suffering.

"Ok," you may say, "but what about the line that says, 'No creation of suffering or noble path to end suffering.' That's what the Four Noble Truths, the most central of the Buddha's teachings, is all about. It makes no sense."

Again, you have to consider the context. The sutra is talking about one who perceives the emptiness of all five skandhas and thus is free of doubt and suffering. Well, if you are at that stage of your practice, then there is no creation of suffering or noble path to end suffering. Suffering for such individuals does not exist.

This is the promise of the Buddhist path, and it is not just available to the enlightened. As I state at other places in this book, for most of us the experience of the Buddhist path is incremental. We do not become enlightened in a flash. Indeed, we may never reach full enlightenment, always remaining at some stage just short of it. But as we progress on the path, we experience more and more the freedom from thought that is described in the sutra and the peace that comes with it.

3.

I moved back to Chicago in 2006 and returned to the Korean Zen temple where I had originally been introduced to Buddhism, going each Sunday morning for the meditation sitting and dharma talk. It felt in many ways like coming home. It was a wonderful experience to meditate and practice with a group of people in such a setting, and I received much good teaching.

Then, early in March of 2007, a Buddhist acquaintance told me that *Tricycle Magazine* (a magazine about Buddhism) was promoting a 28-day at-home retreat. He was going to do it and he wondered whether I would be interested; we could support each other in this effort.

When I checked out the details in the magazine, my first reaction was that this retreat really wouldn't help me, that my practice was already quite disciplined, in the sense that I practiced daily. But then I thought about it more carefully and realized that the retreat would actually add various levels of discipline to my daily practice and that it might indeed be helpful.

For I had been standing at a crossroad for some time ... despite my commitment to jump off the precipice, I still had not been able to surrender my ego to my true Buddha nature. Yes, I was still stuck in the same place despite the teaching of Huyen Te and Thai Tue. My practice had deepened, my awareness had increased, I observed most things without the intervention of thought, but there remained a barrier, certainly as to my core issues ... I was still not one with my true Buddha nature. And so I decided to do the retreat.

My daily practice for years had consisted of a walking and sitting meditation in the morning, about 15 and 30 minutes respectively, shortly after I got up. But often the meditation was not disciplined, as I would fall into focused

THE SELF IN NO SELF

thought on some current issue of mine. I sat quietly, yes, but my thought was engaged; I was not an observer.

The retreat took me back to the basics. The first week, there was a 30-minute morning and evening sitting meditation; during the rest of the day I carried on with my normal daily activities. During the meditations, I observed only my breath and the sounds around me; my mind was silent except for the occasional random thought that passed through (what Huyen Te referred to as "our unfinished business") but to which I did not attach.

Already after the first week, I felt a deepening of my practice and an increase in calm and peace. The second week was basically the same, with a walking meditation added during the day.

The third week, the morning and evening sitting meditation periods were increased to 45 minutes. This was a good stretch for me because it required me to deal with the restlessness and physical discomfort that often comes when sitting for longer periods of time. I would recognize those feelings or sensations, greet them, and then let them go.

During the fourth week, I decided to use part of my sitting meditation time to concentrate on various basic tenets of Buddhism so as to gain a deeper understanding. One day I also focused on loneliness. These were not focused meditations in the sense of my previous daily meditation practice where I was actively engaged in thought. Instead, I just put a concept out there and without thinking let my mind explore its essence.

The final day of the retreat was a total silent retreat from sunrise to sunset. I did four or five 45-minute sitting meditations and several walking meditations. During the rest of the day I either read Buddhist literature or sat silently.

One of the books I read that final retreat day was a section of Sogyal Rinpoche's *Tibetan Book of Living and Dying* that I hadn't read previously. This was my first exposure to the Tibetan practice of "tonglen," giving and receiving ... taking on the suffering and pain of others and giving them your happiness, well-being, and peace of mind.

Sogyal Rinpoche recommends starting this practice by first doing it for yourself. Before one can have such compassion for others, one has to have compassion for oneself. The first step is to *"unseal the spring of loving kindness."* To do that he suggests going back in your mind and recreate, almost visualize, a love that someone gave you that really moved you. My mind wandered through several possibilities both in my adult life and childhood, when suddenly I remembered an instance with my father that was repeated often when I was small ... it was the story I told earlier about him coming to my bed at night when he would get home and playing with my toes.

When I remembered that episode, which had long since been forgotten, I cried because of the love that I was feeling from my father and almost simultaneously a big smile formed on my face. Rinpoche says that, *"You will remember then that even though you may not always feel that you have been loved enough, you were loved genuinely once. Knowing that now will make you feel again that you are, as that person made you feel then, worthy of love and really lovable."* And so it did.

Under his further instruction, I let my heart open and the love that flowed from it was extended to my father, to my family and friends, and to all people. I visualized holding my father as he was dying (I was not there in fact) and saying to him, "You can let go now for I know that you love me and I love you ... I will be ok." I was now ready to practice tonglen on myself.

Rinpoche suggests, for the purpose of this exercise, dividing yourself into two aspects ... one is the aspect of you that is whole, compassionate, etc., the other is the aspect of you that has been hurt, that feels misunderstood, bitter or angry, *"who might have been unjustly treated or abused as a child, or has suffered in relationships or been wronged by society."* As you breathe in, the first aspect opens its heart completely and receives all of the other aspect's pain and suffering. As you breathe out, the first aspect gives the other aspect all its healing love, warmth, trust, and happiness. In response, the other aspect opens its heart to this love and all pain and suffering melt away in this embrace.

What could be more appropriate for me given my history, I thought! And so, I practiced tonglen on myself with beneficial results. Indeed, as the weeks and months passed after the retreat, I practiced both the visualization of my father's love, as well as tonglen on myself, on a regular basis. Each time I did, I felt that smile ... the smile of happiness and love ... form naturally and for many weeks tears would roll down my cheek. Clearly, this was a very cathartic experience for me.

The last breakthrough, which probably built on these exercises I had done, came when I was reading the Heart Sutra. I suddenly realized that I had been reading the language about being at one with all things and experiencing things directly without the intervention of thought as applying to things outside of my self.

While I had for a long time been aware of the illusory nature of all my perceptions and feelings about my self, I had never applied the teaching of the Heart Sutra to my self ... I had not been at one with my self and did not experience my self without the intervention of thought. I had surrendered my ego to my true Buddha nature on every subject other than my self. I knew at that instant that that was why despite all my progress, my core suffering had continued.

What a shock. Let me clarify. I had known that I wasn't at one with my true Buddha nature, else why would I still be suffering. But I hadn't understood why. The realization that I had come to be at one with most things but not with my own self and that I hadn't even realized my restricted reading of the Heart Sutra was painful.

After this realization, I immediately meditated on being at one with my self, my true Buddha nature, and experiencing my self without the intervention of thought. It was another cathartic experience and I cried.

Looking back on it now, it's ironic that I was in the same position as the Zen master described in *The New York Times* article I referred to earlier who lacked any feeling of unity with himself and so went to see a psychiatrist. I had fallen into the same trap; I just hadn't processed it intellectually as he had and hadn't understood why (in the larger sense, not the immediate) until I started writing the section, "The Self in No Self," partly at the impetus of his experience.

The result of this final week and final day of my at-home retreat was that, for the first time, I knew that *all* things are impermanent and that *all* perceptions are illusory ... not just intellectually but at the core of my being. I surrendered *all* aspects of my ego to my true Buddha nature and was at one with myself and all things. When I read various Buddhist texts on the final day, texts that I had read and underlined many times before, I read them with a deep understanding that I had never had before. And I was at least for that moment, that day, free at last of loneliness and rejection because I knew those labels for what they were ... just labels that were products of my mind, not reflections of reality. I was free of my ego.

I could tell in the following days that I was interacting with things and people ... whether it was panhandlers on the street, homeless people in the park, or thinking about the people who slaughtered their neighbors and strangers in Rwanda ... on a different level, in a different way. I understood my oneness with them and felt great compassion for them as human beings rather than fear and revulsion or pity. I was aware of their suffering, that we are all products of our environment.

THE SELF IN NO SELF

Who am I?

I am the tree I see,
The flower that blooms,
The morning rain,
And the cold night air.

I am the bird in flight,
The wounded bear,
The howling wolf,
And the dog lying before the fire.

I am the laughing child,
The old lady begging,
The dope addict,
And the forgetful old man.

I am all things,
And I am nothing

Written on the final day of my at-home retreat, April 14, 2007

Epilogue
The Present

How different my life is now from what it's been for most of my life. In the past, viewed from the outside, my life appeared to most people to be successful on all levels, professional and personal, and yet I experienced inner turmoil and suffering every day. It was never far from me and tainted every positive experience that I had.

Now, viewed from the outside, my life may appear in some disarray. I don't know what I'm going to do with this next phase of my life, professionally or personally, because I am aware of the impermanence of all things and am present in the moment. And yet inwardly, precisely for that reason, I have great peace and calm and experience joy and happiness on a regular basis. I have surrendered my ego to my true Buddha nature and have glimpses of my true self, my lost child … not every moment of every day, but many moments of many days.

I know that my ego is still part of me, just waiting for a moment of weakness to arise, but that's ok … I am aware. And when it arises I "speak" to it as the Buddha would speak to Mara, telling it that I am free of all unskillful desires and that it has no more power over my life. And then it subsides.

I realized recently though that I had one more barrier to cross. The classic Chinese poem "Affirming Faith in Mind" says:

*In this true world of Emptiness
both self and other are no more.
To enter this true empty world,
immediately affirm "not-two."
In this "not-two" all is the same,
with nothing separate or outside.*[48]

After a lifetime of feeling separate from most others, I had thought that with the compassion I now had for all people and things, being usually self-less in my actions, feeling at one with all things in the sense that we are all in this boat of the world together and have the commonality of our samsara and our true Buddha natures, and experiencing things for the most part directly without the intervention of thought having surrendered my ego to my true Buddha nature, that I had crossed the barrier of "not-two," which limits further progress on the path.

But recently when a friend was talking about feeling that he doesn't belong anywhere, I thought about my own experiences past and present. And I realized that while I do feel that in coming and going I never leave home ... I carry my home with me wherever I am because my home, my refuge, is the Buddha, my faith in his teachings, and my meditation practice ... I nevertheless felt separate from my surroundings; I felt I did not belong. I could not say "not-two."

My initial reaction was that with all one reads in the news each day about the extent of hatred and evil in the world, and the past social rejections and hurt I had myself experienced, it would be hard to feel "not-two" even while having compassion for those who have such feelings or commit such acts and loving them unconditionally. I said to myself that this feeling of self and other does not come from thought, it comes from a direct awareness of the facts

---

[48] Roshi Philip Kapleau, op. cit.

of life; even regarding my personal life, I knew what was illusion and what was real. Nevertheless this feeling of separateness, which I had not been so acutely aware of for some time, unsettled me.

Then one morning, something I had recently re-read in Krishnamurti[49] came to mind ... "fear is thought." And I suddenly realized that I had taken those directly experienced facts and turned them into thoughts, and the thoughts created fear. But it was at such a low level of intensity that I wasn't even aware of it until my friend made that statement which caused me to reflect on my own feelings about my surroundings. There is still so much to be learned ... or better put, to be mindful of.

This fear had held me back from interaction with others, strangers, for most of my life (with the one definite exception being the period after my at-home retreat just discussed). Now that I had discerned that and meditated on it, I felt free of that fear and was able to relate to my surroundings and people without that barrier. What a gift!

It has been almost two years since I began writing this book and it has been a journey that I am grateful for. I know that I can never be the carefree person that smiles at me from those photos of me as a toddler for I have observed and learned too much about the world. But I have rediscovered the unconditional love for myself and the unconditional love and compassion for those around me and indeed for all sentient beings that that child ... the embodiment of my true Buddha nature ... felt. And for the most part I observe and experience myself and the world without the intervention of thought. I have returned to my self-nature.

I don't know at this point where all of this will lead. And I'm not really concerned about that. I feel strongly that if I live each day well, the future will take care of itself. In

---

[49] J. Krishnamurti, op. cit.

the meantime, I live with my best friend which each day brings an abundance of love and wonderful moments of joy, laughter, companionship and sharing, I practice the piano, I read, I expand my mind, I have compassion for myself, I have compassion for and help others, I go for walks observing nature and wildlife ... and of course I meditate. I live a good and full life today in the present. What more can one ask for?

www.ingramcontent.com/pod-product-compliance
Lightning Source LLC
Chambersburg PA
CBHW051652040426
42446CB00009B/1100